The Elman Induction

The Elman

Induction

by Graham Old

The Elman Induction

Preface

The current work is the latest instalment in our popular *Inductions Masterclass* series. The aim of the series is to take a popular induction and devote an entire book to discussing its practice. This is something that remains surprisingly rare.

However, this series of books also takes the induction as a starting-point and uses it to teach a series of principles that are beneficial for the wider practice of hypnosis.

This title in the series takes a slightly different approach to its predecessors. We have chosen to unpack the induction strictly according to the stages of its operation. We will look at the importance of viewing the Elman induction as a dynamic process, rather than a prescriptive pattern to be followed. In that sense, it felt slightly counter-intuitive to impose our own pre-designed structure to the book. Instead, we are taking our direction from the the process itself, as taught by Dave Elman.

So, although previous books in this series have taught some elements of an induction, then shared some wider principles that can be drawn out of it, then taught a bit more of the induction and so on, this book is unique. We will simply outline the order of events as demonstrated in the Elman Induction. However, we will draw out the principles that can be extrapolated from the induction as we proceed, as we suggest different understandings of what is taking place and why it works. Hopefully, this will cause the current book to have an organic feel to it, as nothing is forced into the induction simply to serve as a teaching aid.

One point we will make a number of times in this book is that you do not need to share Elman's understanding of how his induction works in order to use it effectively. That is equally true with our understanding. If you have read other books in the *Inductions Masterclass* series, then you will know that we are not interested in pushing academic theories for their own sake. Neither are we concerned with promoting any particular school or model of hypnosis. So, although we recognise that the Elman Induction is often taught as reliant on Elman's definition of hypnosis and theories of depth of hypnosis, we wanted to see if it was possible to faithfully teach the induction in the way that Elman taught it, without necessarily being tied to his wider model.

Our intention, as always, is incredibly simple: we seek to take inductions that work and enable you to work with them. If you feel that you can most effectively use the Elman induction as a thorough devotee of Elman and his theories, we are confident that this book will enable you to do so. Similarly, if you feel no connection to the model that Elman presented, but still want to use his induction, this book should support you to do that and more.

Acknowledgements

I am grateful to H. Larry Elman, son of Dave Elman, for reading an earlier version of this book and offering his comments. I am especially grateful for his thoughts on those areas where we disagree regarding his father's work.

In addition, I am grateful to Melissa Tiers and Sean Michael Andrews for their time, attention and kind feedback.

All Rights Reserved

Disclaimer

This work is meant as a discussion of one way to approach the Dave Elman induction. Specifically, it follows the argument of Larry Elman in insisting that his father's famous induction is a process to go through, not a script to be recited. We take this idea further and demonstrate that the Elman Induction serves as a good example of the concept of *Therapeutic Inductions*, first discussed in our *The Anatomy of Inductions*.

We are offering a model for consideration, investigation and conversation. No part of this work is meant as a replacement for proper training in effective hypnosis or psychotherapy.

Please be aware that any experimentation with the ideas presented in this document is undertaken at your own risk and responsibility. At all times when practicing hypnosis, it is your responsibility to ensure that you comply with the laws and regulations of your home country, region, state or territory.

Contents

Introduction

The Dave Elman Induction is widely regarded as one of the most effective and easily learned inductions available[1]. It promises to allow even the novice hypnotist to take anyone into a deep state of hypnosis in little more than 3 minutes. Yet, where did it come from and what is its intended purpose?

Dave Elman

Dave Elman was born Dave Kopelman on May 6, 1900 in North Dakota, USA. He first developed an interest in hypnosis when, aged 8, a travelling hypnotist helped his father find pain relief from the Cancer that would eventually take his life.

In his early teens, in order to support his mother and five siblings, Dave worked odd jobs and developed something of a reputation as a musician, entertainer and comedian. He later joined the vaudeville circuit, where he was billed as 'The World's Youngest and Fastest Hypnotist'. It is at this point that Elman changed his name from Kopelman, as the longer name took up too much space on billboards.

Elman eventually moved into radio work and he was so

---

1 See http://www.howtodoinductions.com/inductions/elman.

successful in this arena that when he took a vacation in 1939, it was Eleanor Roosevelt – at the time, the wife of the US President – who accepted the invitation to stand in for him. The show that the First Lady was a temporary replacement host for was Elman's popular 'Hobby Lobby', where members of the public would come in to talk about their hobbies and try to win the vote of an invited celebrity.

After a hypnotist came on his show, Elman's wife told him that he could have done a better job and before long he was doing just that. He later dedicated his life to teaching hypnosis to doctors and dentists. The course that he taught proved so popular that the content was published as a book in 1964, originally titled, *Findings in Hypnosis*. That book, later re-published as *Hypnotherapy*, has rightly established Elman as one of the greats in the world of Hypnosis.

The Dave Elman Induction(s)

Dave Elman never taught 'the Elman induction'. In fact, he goes to great lengths in his book to argue that there are countless inductions and that anything can be used to induce hypnosis. To prove the point, he then demonstrates that not only can *anything* be used, but even 'nothing' can be used, proven by the fact that he achieves eye-closure with a group of course participants without saying a word![2]

The induction that today goes by the name *The Elman Induction* is simply referenced by Elman himself as 'the

---

2 Elman, Dave. (1977). *Hypnotherapy*. Glendale, CA: Westwood Publishing Co. pp. 57-60.

repeated induction technique'.[3] Elman viewed this as a way to lead someone into a deep state of hypnosis – which he called 'somnambulism' – within 3 minutes. In fact, 3 minutes was for beginners. Elman soon expected his students to reach somnambulism, using the process he had created, within 60 seconds.

We will later discuss the concept of somnambulism and different depths and states of hypnosis. However, for now I will simply say that it is not essential for you to believe everything that Dave Elman believed to achieve great results using his process. If you have read any of our previous works, in particular *The Anatomy of Inductions*, then you will know that we do not take a position on the debates over trance and State that have divided hypnotists for hundreds of years. Instead, we focus on the experience itself and I am confident that as you read on – regardless of your particular model or school or hypnosis – you will find that the 'Elman induction' is an incredibly simple, quick and reliable means to lead someone into a 'deep' experience of hypnosis.

Where are we Going?

We will begin where Elman began by looking at the concept of Consent and its role within Hypnosis in the 21st Century. We will then move on to consider the argument of Dave Elman's youngest son, Larry, who passionately argues for a re-appreciation of the Elman Induction as a process, not a static script. This may seem like an obvious point to some, or an irrelevant one to others. However, we consider it essential to the proper execution of the induction.

---

3 Elman, Dave. (1977). P. 102.

From there, we will break down the induction into its various parts, looking at each aspect of the process in turn. As with the other books in the *Inductions Masterclass* series, our aim is not merely to teach individual inductions, but to use them as a doorway into the deeper principles and practice of hypnosis. So, each aspect of the process will be explored as a spring-board to teaching wider principles that you will find useful in your practice of hypnosis.

We start by exploring Dave Elman's understanding of hypnosis and the unique way he achieved eye-closure. Here we will also discuss the notion of 'Priority of Thought', a useful idea borrowed from Brief Hypnosis.

Then we will look at the natural brief deepeners that can be employed at the early stages of the Elman Induction. At this point and throughout the book, we will provide transcripts of the principles in action.

The discussion will move on to look at Elman's utilisation of fractionation, which will clarify the reason that he called this process 'the repeated induction technique'.

Following that, we will look at the 'arm-drop' used in the Elman induction and argue that, like each stage of the process, it can serve a dual function.

Without seeking to get lost in controversy for controversy's sake, we move on to 'losing the numbers' and take a look at the concept of Somnambulism and depths of hypnosis. We will argue, with respect, that Elman's understanding of his process is not a necessary component in its successful delivery.

Finally, we will provide a trouble-shooting section where we address some of the most common questions that arise with the practice of the Elman induction.

There are numerous exercises to be completed

throughout the book, to practically reinforce the information presented. These are an essential part of the book, not to be skipped over or underestimated. Our hope is that reading this book is as close to a live training as you can get without leaving your home. So, the training contained in these pages has something of a modular feel, each section building on what has gone before, as you progress in your knowledge and practice of the Elman Induction.

Of course, it is completely up to the reader to decide how much time and effort they wish to devote to the exercises, or applying the learning from one chapter before moving on to the next. However, we strongly believe that you will get far more out of this book if you treat it as a training manual to put in to practice and learn from, rather than merely an information guide.

A Further Note on Terminology used

Throughout this book, you will find us referring to 'trance' and at times using terminology such as 'subconscious', deepening, somnambulism, being 'under' hypnosis and so on. Please bear in mind that these are phenomenological descriptions, merely meant to convey what the hypnotee may be experiencing.

As already noted, we are not endorsing any particular interpretation of hypnosis, or taking sides in the perennial debates over the nature of trance or the existence of a special hypnotic state.

At various points throughout the book, we may refer to those experiencing hypnosis as 'patients'. This is not to imply that the Elman induction is only useful in a medical setting, or should only be employed by medical practitioners. It merely reflects Dave Elman's own terminology, which was fitting for the setting he was teaching in.

EXERCISE

Consider times in the past when you have hypnotised someone. Or, give some thought to times when you plan to hypnotise someone in the future.

What was/is your aim in hypnotising them?

There is no right or wrong answer here. You might have hypnotised them to remove a phobia, or help them overcome some other personal issue. Or, perhaps you simply intended to give someone an interesting experience.

Now, consider what your aim was/is in using an induction, whichever one you used.

Did you use the induction to get them into hypnosis? Or to increase their suggestibility? Or to demonstrate the power of hypnosis, or something else?

What do you think of Elman's intention in using the induction we are discussing in this book to lead someone into somnambulism?

GRAHAM OLD

Elman in the 21st Century

Authority, Control and Consent

There were 2 indisputable giants of Hypnosis in the 20th Century, Milton Erickson and Dave Elman. The differences between them are as interesting as they are enlightening. Erickson was a respected M.D. who wrote numerous books and papers on hypnosis and the induction of hypnosis. His followers did much to build his reputation, even whilst he was alive, by publishing papers and books on Erickson's techniques and his celebrated indirect approach.

By Contrast, Elman was a former radio presenter and vaudeville performer, who wrote one book outlining his very direct approach. His reputation depended almost solely upon his lectures and the impact that his course had upon the doctors and dentists who attended. Compared to Erickson, Elman was somewhat short on theory, focusing instead on practical principles that enabled medical professionals to do their jobs more effectively and improved the lives of the children, families and adults they worked with.

Occasionally, it has been said that Elman was so effective because he worked in an age when people showed respect to Doctors and those in authority. More so than today, people trusted medical practitioners almost unquestioningly so. It therefore makes sense that the instructions of a Hypnotist, or medical professionals using hypnosis – perceived to be authority figures – would be accepted and acted on with little resistance.

Although this argument may seem reasonable, it falls at the first hurdle. Elman is clear, from the very beginning, that his process is one of consent. That may appear to support the argument above, yet it pays to recognise that consent and submission are not the same thing. Elman teaches that 'all hypnosis is self-hypnosis' and that hypnosis is a process whereby the hypnotee allows the hypnotist to pilot their dreams. However, at no point do they give up autonomy and neither do they come under the control of anyone else.

Elman writes:

> 'As a practitioner employing this tool, all you can ever do is to show a patient how to go over the hurdle from a normal waking or sleeping state into the peculiar state of mind known as hypnosis. You won't hypnotize him; he will hypnotize himself. This means that those of us using suggestion yield no "power" over any subject.'[4]

Elsewhere, Elman emphatically states that even in the so-called 'coma' state, the patient retains ultimate control and could snap out of trance if they were presented with suggestions they found unpalatable.[5]

It is perhaps helpful if we view consent not as the counterpart of control, but of co-operation. As Sean

---

4 ibid., p. ix.
5 ibid., p. 134.

Michael Andrews puts it, hypnosis is a dance in which the hypnotist takes the lead.[6] So, although Elman's model might position the hypnotist as an authority, it is not an absolute authority. Instead, it is a temporary role that he plays with the patient's permission, at the appropriate time, for a specific purpose. Interestingly, there are points within the Elman induction, where the patient is instructed not to help and to let the hypnotist do the work. Yet, there are other places where the patient may be instructed that they need to do this for themselves. This highlights the idea that 'taking the lead' is not necessarily bound to the idea of being an authority figure – thus denying the idea that it is an inappropriate or unattainable idea for today's world.

We might illustrate this with the image of someone having a driving lesson. They remain in the Driving seat, in full control of the vehicle, which they may theoretically stop any time they feel the need. However, for the duration of the lesson, they acknowledge someone else as their teacher and choose to go along with their directions. The idea is not one of surrender or absolute authority. It is about co-operation and playing the part allotted to them by the situation.

All of this might suggest that the model of authority and consent seen in the Elman Induction is actually particularly apt for the world today. We see two partners engaged in a dance, with set roles and mutually agreed expectations. The dance will only work if each party plays their part and respects the co-operative nature of their joint endeavour. At the very most, this is a functional authority that anyone who has been to school, or paid for

---

6 Patterson, D. *"The Dave Elman Induction"* [DVD]. The Atlantic Hypnosis Institute.

an item in a shop, or accepted a prescription from a Doctor, or followed the directions of a Yoga instructor will be more than familiar with. We are not talking about control or surrender, but co-operation and partnership.

Perhaps Elman and Erickson were not always as far apart as their respective followers often imply!

Process, not Script

Whilst we are looking at the Elman Induction in the 21st Century, we would do well to consider how the induction is often taught today.

There is an unfortunate trend in modern hypnotherapy to reduce the art of hypnosis to manageable chunks and transferable scripts. As a teaching-tool, this is perfectly natural and makes sense. Many people feel more able to understand a concept if they can see its component parts broken down and outlined in a logical manner. The trouble comes when these outlines are then taken to be the core of the 'technique'. In the end, we face a situation where the codified list of steps are what is passed-on and the heart of the art is lost.

Of course, there is nothing wrong with showing an overview of a process or method, or breaking down an event into a series of steps. This can be helpful to provide a clear summary of the bigger picture, before delving into the details and exploring the nuances and subtleties of what took place. In one sense, this book is an example of such a practice. The problem occurs when the overview – or even a detailed list of steps – is presented as the essence of the event.

Now, I should perhaps clarify that I am not saying no hypnotist should ever read or utilise scripts. I am aware that many people find them useful as a memory aid in the early days of practice. Moreover, it makes sense that in your preparation for seeing a client, you might decide you want to include a particular phrase in an exact way. Additionally, there may be certain parabolic stories that you employ on a number of occasions, or specific words that you almost always use, perhaps to bring someone out of hypnosis for example. It could be said therefore that we all use scripts; it is simply the case that we have internalised them through regular use.

However, I would still argue that the use of scripts for induction purposes – particularly in the case of the Elman Induction – is a negative rather than a positive development.[7] The main reason why I say that induction scripts, or at least an *over-dependence* on them, are a negative is because they potentially take our eyes off of what is happening in front of us. I implore all new hypnotists – and especially therapeutic hypnotists – to get into the habit of reading their clients over and above reading scripts. The narrative you need to be involved with is not the static list in your hand, but the living person in front of you.

By paying greater attention to the interaction between yourself, your client and their inner world, you will be better prepared to handle unexpected reactions or unforeseen responses. If you go into a session with an over-reliance on your script, how will you develop the flexibility to respond when your client veers off of the

---

7 Readers may be forgiven for wondering how I can say this
   when I am the developer of the popular website
   howtodoinductions.com. Is that not a collection of induction
   scripts? On the contrary, the site intends to provide a
   selection of transcripts of inductions in action, not scripts to
   be blindly followed.

script?

Additionally, I have myself seen a hypnotherapist who read from scripts. Not only was this immediately obvious from their reading voice – and do not underestimate how difficult it is to hide the fact that you're reading – but when I opened my eyes at the end, I saw them closing their book and putting it back on the shelf. Any credibility they had gained during the session was instantly lost. Nothing speaks 'amateur' and 'out of your depth' more than a therapist who relies on regurgitating the words of others to be able to speak to the fellow human being sat in front of them. When we remember Elman's description of the hypnotist as a pilot, or guide, into hypnosis, we cannot afford to lose credibility in this way.

So it is that Larry Elman argues strongly for a fresh appreciation of his father's induction as a process.[8] Elman Jr. suggests that a script approach to the Elman Induction should be avoided for the following reasons:

- Scripts do not show how or why something works
- You lose credibility, as clients can tell you are reading
- You can come across as insincere
- Scripts do not prepare for the unexpected
- You lose flexibility.[9]

All of this is perhaps secondary to the fact that Dave Elman himself explicitly taught a process, based on a number of principles, with a specific goal in mind. He did not produce a script. Therefore, through the rest of this

8 Elman, H. Larry. (2011). *Blueprint of the Dave Elman Induction.* Henderson, NC: Dave Elman Hypnosis Institute.
9 Elman, H. Larry. (2011). Pp.5-14.

book we will look at each part in the process, to understand what is happening, how and why.

EXERCISE

Many people feel that Elman benefited from the cultural expectation that respect was shown to Doctors and those in authority.

What do you make of the argument in this chapter that this is not a necessary component of the Elman induction?

In what ways might you arouse respect from those you are working with, without having to be seen as an authority?

The Elman Process

Having said all that we have about scripts, we will now risk appearing to contradict ourselves by providing an outline of the process! However, it should be obvious that this is offered as a glimpse of the bigger picture, to enable you to then delve deeper.

- Pre-talk

- Eye Closure

- Deepeners

- Fractionation

- Arm Drop

- Losing the Numbers

As we proceed, it should become obvious that this list is offered somewhat tongue-in-cheek. This is how the process may look most of the time, particularly if the induction is performed verbatim from a script.

However, as we unpack each stage of the process, you will see that the details of the induction may look different each time it is executed. Understanding what is really happening will afford you the flexibility and freedom to follow the process as Elman intended, but to adapt the stages as appropriate.

For that reason, this process is offered as something of a teaser, as we are aware that it is how many people would recognise the Elman Induction. After we have looked at things in more depth, we will then provide a more accurate and faithful summary of the process, before trouble-shooting the induction in practice.

EXERCISE

Jump ahead and read some of the transcripts in this book.

Or visit www.howtodoinductions.com and search for the Elman induction. Alternatively, search for videos of the induction online.

Break the induction down into its various parts. See which aspects you consider to be essential.

Do your parts match with the process as it is outlined above?

Take some time to consider why the induction is staged like it is. Why, for example, does the fractionation not come before the deepeners?

GRAHAM OLD

The Pre-talk

Let's start at the beginning, with the pre-talk and set-up. As he taught his process, Elman did not always use a pre-talk. In fact, at times he explicitly advocates avoiding talk of hypnosis altogether.[10] However, it is worth bearing in mind that Elman was teaching Doctors and Dentists, not hypnotists. He taught them to tell their patients that they were going to share a quick method for relaxing rapidly. The assumption is that patients would presume this was part of the medical procedure and would accept it as readily as they would follow any other instruction designed to help them.

However, things are quite different for most hypnosis practitioners in the 21st Century. For the majority of us, people who come to see us are aware that we use hypnosis and may have what Elman calls, 'the fear associated with the word in the minds of the uninformed.'[11] It therefore makes sense that we would address these fears, so that we can proceed with the necessary level of consent and appropriate co-operation.

---

10 Elman (1977), p. 36.
11 ibid.

The Nature of Hypnosis

Before we discuss the kind of pre-talk that might fit with the Elman Induction, it would make sense to briefly look at Elman's understanding of hypnosis and also what he saw as the 5 signs of someone being in hypnosis.

We will look at Elman's definition of hypnosis in more depth when we come to his approach to eye-closure. For now, the following quote will suffice:

> 'Hypnosis is a state of mind in which the critical faculty of the human mind is bypassed, and selective thinking established.'[12]

The 'critical faculty' is understood to mean that part of your mind that passes judgement and distinguishes between hot and cold, sweet and sour, and so on. I have seen it described as a guard dog that stands between the conscious mind and the subconscious mind. In this model, it has the power to accept or reject suggestions from entering the subconscious mind.

This can be a useful concept to explain how hypnosis enables people to take on new ideas and see things from a fresh perspective. However, we need to note that patients who are especially nervous of the Hypnotist taking control, may find the idea of losing this protective part of their mind slightly disconcerting.

Signs of Hypnosis

Elman taught that when someone is in hypnosis, they give off five signs. He considered these signs to be minute

---

12 ibid., p. 26.

and easily missed, which is another reason that hypnotists may want to pay more attention to their clients and less to scripts.

Here are Elman's five signs of hypnosis:

1. Body warmth
2. Fluttering of the eyelids
3. Increased lacrimation
4. Whites of the eyes getting red or pinkish
5. Eyeballs going up into the head.

Elman's list has some overlap with the 'minimal cues of trance' often sought out by Ericksonian hypnotists. We have discussed this at length elsewhere.[13] This is not the place to question the scientific veracity of Elman's signs or the Ericksonian minimal cues. It may well be that these are instead symptoms of relaxation or the result of eye-fixation. However, for now, we can accept that they are a part of Elman's model and can be a useful sign that things are progressing as expected.

Pre-talk

Elman taught that the three requisites for hypnosis are:

- The consent of the subject
- Communication between the operator and the subject
- Freedom from fear, or reluctance on the subject's part to trust the operator.[14]

---

13 Mastering the Leisure Induction, pp.69-72.
14 Elman, (1977), p. xiii.

It is therefore good practice for an Elmanian pre-talk to address these issues. For example, you may want to structure a pre-talk to include the following points.

You are not under the hypnotist's control. It is surprising how many people still operate under this misconception of hypnosis, helped in no small part by movies and media representations of the subject of hypnosis.

Following on from the previous point, it is beneficial to emphasise *the role of consent*. You might want to make it clear that you and your patient are partners in this process and that at no point can you make them do anything they do not want to do. Instead, you are relying on them to let you guide them into hypnosis.

Some people have a fear that it is possible to get stuck in hypnosis. This may be the result of seeing people slumped over in stage hypnosis shows. You can reassure them that *it is not possible to get stuck in hypnosis*, whilst making the suggestion that the experience is so enjoyable that they may wish that they could!

I have come across a surprising number of people who fear that they will blurt out their deepest secrets under hypnosis. It pays to remind them that hypnosis is a consent state and that *they will reject any suggestions that appear immoral or unwise to them*, including revealing their deepest darkest secrets. In Elman's model, people do not do anything under hypnosis that they would not do in their waking state.

Finally, this is the point to *ask for permission to touch them*. This does not need to be any more awkward than you make it. If you appear nervous, you are going to make your hypnotee wonder why and then question your motives. My advice is to act almost blasé, as if you are asking them permission to talk to them. In fact, following advice given by Jonathan Chase, I ask for permission to touch *whilst touching them*! Simply touch them on the back of the wrist whilst saying:

> "A times, I may touch you here, or here [touch the forearm], or here [touch the elbow] or here [touch the shoulder].
>
> "Okay?"

I do not ask if this is okay with an uncertain or insecure tone of voice. It is more correct to say that I state it as a matter of fact. With the whole request, I act as if I am asking a perfectly normal question and I presume that they are going to give me the go ahead. And they always do.

EXERCISE

Write an example pre-talk that addresses each of the concerns discussed in this chapter. Review it and consider which parts you may want to remove or adapt, depending on who you are working with.

Then proceed to read the following example pre-talk and adjust your example to include any elements you find helpful.

An Example Pre-talk

Hypnotist: "Before we start, I would just like to address some misconceptions that people sometimes have about hypnosis.

"If we're going to proceed, it will be good to know that we're on the same page. Right?"

Client: "Yeah."

H: "Okay, well the first thing to address is probably the idea of control. You know, that old idea that hypnosis worked because the hypnotist controlled a subject to do their bidding?"

C: [Smiles]

H: "This is the kind of thing we see in Hollywood movies and it could not be further removed from reality. What really happens in hypnosis is that you are actually *more* in control than usual. After all, what we are after is enabling you to re-gain control of those thoughts and behaviours that are currently troubling you."

C: "Yeah."

H: "Some people think that you become a zombie, or just zonk-out completely, but it's not like that. Actually, you may find that your hearing is sharpened and your imagination is increased. Some people have even described hypnosis as a state of *enhanced* awareness. What you'll probably experience is more like the first few minutes when you wake up in the morning and you're just floating in that hazy space between being not quite awake but not really asleep. Or, like when you day-dream and your mind just drifts off to some other place. You're still safe and in control and could snap yourself out of it any time you chose to. (But the truth is that you're so relaxed that you just don't want to!)

"Or, those times you have when you're driving on a familiar route and your conscious mind kinda takes a back seat. And when you get home, you're left thinking, 'how did I get here?!'

"Rather than giving up control, think of hypnosis as a process of giving consent, or agreeing to co-operate. You allow me to guide your imagination and agree to follow certain suggestions – but only those suggestions that you are happy to follow and that are designed for your good. This is precisely why some hypnotists say that 'All Hypnosis is self-hypnosis'. In effect, all I am doing is joining you on a journey, offering directions and pointing out the sights along the way."

C: [Nods.]

H: "At no point will you do or say anything that you don't want to do. Hypnosis is not a truth serum and you will not give me your bank PIN code or cluck like a chicken – unless that's something you particularly want to do!

"Finally, you can not get stuck in hypnosis. That has never happened and cannot happen. As I've said, you freely choose to give consent; you do not come under my control. What does happen sometimes is that the experience is so enjoyable that you might wish you could get stuck in it, but it doesn't happen. After all, the goal here is to get you out there to carry on with your every-day life, not to entertain you in here indefinitely.

"Oh, one last thing, as we continue, at times I might [touches wrist] touch you here, or here [touches elbow] or here [touches shoulder]. Okay."

C: "Yeah."

EXERCISE

Do you think it is useful to have a pre-written pre-talk that you use with each and every hypnotee you work with? Or is it preferable to tailor it to the individual client?

Is there a risk that a pre-written pre-talk would alert clients to concerns and issues they may not have previously been aware of?

Consider ways that you may be able to make use of your client's nervousness or apprehension? Is it always beneficial to address their concerns, or might you use them to your – and their – advantage?

Find a friend or family member who would be willing to let you practice with them. Discuss any concerns they may have and note how many of them match those discussed above.

GRAHAM OLD

Eye Closure

The role of eye closure and the consequent eye-lock plays a vital role in the Elman Induction. In some approaches to hypnosis, eye-closure is almost seen as the primary goal of hypnotic inductions. For example, I have seen some hypnotists perform a prolonged relaxation induction and then act as if hypnosis has been reached when the patient's eyes finally close. Elman did not share this view.

Eye closure, followed by catalepsy of the eye-lids is, according to Elman, 'the entering wedge' of hypnosis. This is because Elman understood that when you have catalepsy of a group of small muscles – in this case, the eyelids – you have a bypass of the critical faculty. However, you have to go further to secure selective thinking.[15]

The catalepsy of the eyelids, that follows the closure of the eyes, functions as assurance to the hypnotist that the client is engaging with the process. Additionally, it convinces the client that they are entering hypnosis. Finally, it can function to deepen the experience for the client as the credibility of the hypnotist and the credibility of the process is confirmed for them. In this way, the client's expectation is massively increased and the road ahead is smoothed-out in front of you.

This is another reason why I do not believe that

---

15 ibid., pp. 25-27.

Elman's historic social circumstances – the apparent greater respect given to medical professionals – is a hindrance for hypnotists today. The position of a medical practitioner may have increased expectation, as patients were more inclined to believe what they were told. However, within the Elman process, eye-closure and catalepsy is employed at the start, increasing the client's expectation and engagement with the process, whilst providing you with the 'entering wedge' necessary to proceed. Thus, expectation and co-operation is built into the process from the very beginning.

The Elman Handshake

Elman's initial attempts to achieve eye closure (which for him always included the element of a consequent eye-lock), formed the basis for what is sometimes seen as an induction in its own right – the Elman Handshake.

Here is Elman's description of using a handshake to lead up to eye-closure:

> Walk up to the subject and say: "I'm going to shake your hand three times.
>
> "The first time your eyes will get tired... let them.
> "The second time, they'll want to close... let them.
>
> "The third time they will lock and you won't be able to open them... *Want* that to happen, and watch it happen...

"Now, one...

"two... now close your eyes...

"now three... and they're locked and you'll find that they just won't work, no matter how hard you try. The harder you try, the less they'll work.

"Test them, and you'll find they won't work at all..."[16]

There are a number of benefits to an approach that involves a handshake. Very few people will refuse to shake hands, as it is considered a friendly gesture and something of an automatic behaviour pattern in the West. This can be useful in developing rapport.

Additionally, the handshake allows you to assess the temperature of your client. Are they tense? Cold, or warm? Bearing in mind, Elman's signs of hypnosis, you do not want someone who is too hot or too cold. Ideally, a warm hand could imply a receptiveness to you.

The Hand Pass

This technique then evolved into one that utilised a hand-pass to achieve eye closure. Here is how Larry Elman describes the technique:

---

16 ibid., p. 25.

The hypnotist would shake hands with the subject, and then place his hand a few inches above the subject's eyes. The hand would be held horizontally, with palm facing the floor, with the fingers together and positioned only a few inches in front of the subject's nose.

The hand would then be lowered past the person's eyes at a slow but steady pace. Normally, the subject's eyes would be closed by the time the hand reached a point in front of the subject's chin.[17]

The hand is lowered at such a speed to tire the eyes. As the hand is horizontal, the eyes have to focus harder to look at it, causing them to go cross-eyed and be more easily tired. As the hand is lowered, the hypnotist would make suggestions that the eyes are getting tired, pacing it so that the eyes are closing as the hand reaches the chin.

You would then proceed with similar patter to that above, suggesting that the eyes are closed and cannot open.

The Two-Finger Method

Elman then discovered the two-finger eye-closure method, which he described as 'the fastest technique ever devised for obtaining hypnosis.'[18] Here is the technique used on a young girl, by a Dentist that Elman had trained:

---

17 Elman, H.L, (2011), pp. 18-20.
18 Elman, (1977), p. 41.

Dentist: "Jean, I guess you play a lot with your dolls when you're home. And you probably pretend a lot with them, isn't that right? Well, we have a little game of pretend too. And if you can learn to play this little game of pretend, nothing that happens in this dentist's office will bother or disturb you. You won't feel anything that we're doing if you learn to play this little game. Would you like to learn it?"

Patient: "Yes."

Dentist: "All right, open your eyes wide. I'm going to show you this little game. I'm going to pull your eyes shut with my forefinger and my thumb, like this. [Gently places thumb and finger on eyelids and draws them down.] Now you pretend with your whole heart and soul that you can't open your eyes. That's all you have to do. Just pretend that. Now, I will take me hand away [removes hand] and you pretend so hard that when you try to open your eyes they just won't work. Now try to make them work while you're pretending. Try hard. They just won't work, see. Now just because you're pretending like that, anything we do in this office won't bother or disturb you at all. In your mind you can be home playing with your dolls and you won't feel anything I have to do."[19]

The game pretence was particularly fitting for a young

19 ibid., pp.41-42.

child. This enabled them to relax instantly. With an adult, Elman recommended using a more sophisticated approach to bypass the critical faculty, making the instructions to relax more explicit.

> Elman: [Addressing patient]: Every time you come to this office, I notice how tense you get, and if I could teach you how to relax, you wouldn't mind anything we have to do. Suppose I teach you how to relax. Would you like that?

> Patient: Yes.

> Elman: Take a good long breath. Now open your eyes wide. I'm going to pull your eyelids shut with my forefinger and my thumb. Now I want you to relax the muscles that are underneath my fingers. Now I will take my hand away. Relax your eye muscles to the point where they just won't work. Then, when you're sure those eye muscles won't work, test them and make sure they won't work. Test them hard...[20]

The benefit of the two-finger method is that there is something kinaesthetically persuasive about having someone else close your eyes for you. It is a simple difference, but the eyes can feel more firmly shut if someone else has shut them, rather than you just closing them yourself.

---

20 ibid., p.43.

THE ELMAN INDUCTION

Close your Eyes

The induction eventually developed into the version that is most well-known today, simply instructing the client to close their eyes. Nevertheless, there are sometimes benefits to using the more elaborate methods described above. If nothing else, they add an element of the unusual and unexpected to your induction ritual, which serves to convey the idea that something special is happening.

However, when I am using the Elman Induction, I tend to simply invite my clients to close their eyes and take it from there.

> Hypnotist: "I'd like to invite you to close your eyes... And now, become aware of your eyelids and those tiny muscles around the eyes. And relax them completely... completely relaxed. And when you know that those eyelids are so relaxed that you couldn't open your eyes without letting go of that relaxation, go ahead and try and open them... And find that as you try, they simply relax even more, all tension melting away."

If you have never used the Elman Induction before, this catalepsy may seem too simple to be true. However, it relies upon an idea that we call 'Priority of Thought'. Essentially, you invite your client to hold two opposing ideas, or carry out two opposing actions, at the same time. Then, you imply – or even state explicitly – that one of those ideas takes prominence.

Look again at the example with the young girl above.

She is told to pretend that she cannot open her eyes. Yet, she is also told to try to open her eyes. As a child might mistakenly think she is to stop doing one in order to be able to do the other, the Dentist says 'Now try to make them work *while you're pretending*.' He makes it clear to her that she is to carry on performing the first action, whilst then attempting to also simultaneously carry out a second action. This is a simple and effective way to achieve hypnotic phenomena.

Try this out for yourself:

1. Place your hand on your thigh and <u>DO NOT MOVE THAT HAND</u>.

2. Now, whilst obeying the first instruction, go ahead and try as hard as you can to lift your hand up.

If you followed the instructions correctly – and accepted the priority to be given to the first instruction – then you would have had the interesting experience of trying with all of your might to lift your hand off of your leg, but it just would not budge.

This is not the place to go into the Priority of Thought concept in too much detail, or explore the nuances that can make it more effective or less obvious. However, it should be clear that essentially what we see at this early stage of the Elman Induction is a linguistic trick. If that trick is too obvious then it will not function to sufficiently bypass the critical faculty. It will just seem as if the hypnotist is asking you to do something that he's just told you to ensure that you do not do. Yet, if you can frame it as a game, or as a consequence of relaxing well, then it provides you with an effective bypass of the critical faculty and a wedge into hypnosis.

When that bypass of the critical faculty is effective enough then it may automatically lead to selective thinking also. If we turn again to the example with the young child above, the suggestion that nothing the Dentist does will bother her is immediately piggy-backed onto the pretence of her eyes not opening. Both will have been experienced and accepted as the automatic result of her pretending that her eyes cannot open whilst she is playing with her dolls at home.

This works in exactly the same way with adults, though added steps may be needed. Essentially, the simple catalepsy of a group of small muscles – by virtue of Priority of Thought - is used to bypass their critical faculty. They now perceive that the process is working and that you are successfully engaging them to experience a shift in their reality. This prepares them to accept your further suggestions and gradually builds up to selective thinking, which for Elman was when hypnosis was reached.

An added advantage of the Priority of Thought concept is that it offers the reassurance that if your client does open their eyes, then it is clear that they have either i) not understood or ii) intentionally resisted.

How to Begin

Although common descriptions of the Elman induction have it beginning with eye-closure and eye-lock, that is not essential. The process can really begin in any number of ways. Elman chose the catalepsy of a small group of muscles, in this case the eyes, because it is so simple to do. It also leads naturally into relaxation, reinforcing the idea that this is a pleasant experience and allowing clients to lower their guard. However, any easy catalepsy can be chosen, such as inability to raise or lower the little finger, or even something as basic as Magnetic Fingers.[21] The key is to find that simple and straightforward way in which to bypass the critical faculty and begin selective thinking and the suspension of disbelief.

How you frame what you are doing really depends on context and your aims. As seen with the Dentist above, the catalepsy can be presented as the result of relaxation, or the outcome of a game. Additionally, it may be implied that it is a demonstration of the Hypnotist's power, or a revelation of the power of the client's subconscious mind. Finally, it may be seen as a simple example of the power of the process itself.

The transcripts offered throughout this book provide examples of each approach.

---

21 http://howtodoinductions.com/exercises/fingers

EXERCISE

Take some time to consider the Priority of Thought concept. Do you feel that this is a useful addition to your practice of hypnosis? Do you think that your clients would find it useful?

What do you make of the argument in this chapter that Elman's eye-closure relies upon the Priority of Thought?

If you do not find the Priority of Thought a useful concept, begin to work on your own model that allows you to achieve apparently hypnotic phenomena within a similar time-scale. It is more than possible that you will develop a superior model, more suited to you and your approach to hypnosis.

Using Priority of Thought, or your own version, practice achieving the eye-lock with a friend or family member.

GRAHAM OLD

Transcript of the Induction

The following transcript is an example of the Induction in action, offered for analysis, not imitation.

> Hypnotist: "Take a long deep breath, fill up your lungs real good and hold it for a second. Now, as you breathe out, just close your eyes down... And let yourself relax. Getting rid of that surface tension in your body, letting your shoulders relax. And let yourself go.

> "And now, I would like you to put your awareness on your eyelids. And just go ahead and relax those eyes completely. That's it. In fact, I want you to relax them so deeply, that as long as you choose not to remove that relaxation, those eyelids just won't work... You're just too relaxed. And when you know that you've done that, hold on to that relaxation and give them a good test; make sure they won't work... Give them a real good test... That's funny, right? [pause]

> "Now, stop testing and just let yourself relax even more... much much more.

"And that level of relaxation that you have in your eyes, I want you to take that, that same quality of relaxation, bring it up to the top of your head, down the back of you neck... And send it now down through your body from the top of your head to the tip of your toes. Let go of every muscle, every fibre, every nerve... And just drift down, deeper, relaxed. That's it.

"Letting go, letting go, drifting, floating, sinking down...

"Okay, let's really deepen this experience now. In a moment, not yet but in a moment, I'll tell you to open your eyes and then to close them again. And when you close your eyes, you can send a wave of relaxation through your body, from the top of your head to the tip of your toes. And you can relax ten times deeper. Just want it and you can have it. So, open your eyes now... And close your eyes... And really... Let go. 10 times deeper. Feel your body relax, much more. That's perfect.

"In a moment, I'll ask you to open and close your eyes again. This time, when you close your eyes, I want you to double this physical relaxation... Just let it go twice as deep. So, open your eyes... And close them down... Way down... Deeper... Twice as deep... Deeper... Relaxed.

"Okay, so, in a moment – not yet, but in a moment - we'll do that one more time... And notice how easily it occurs this time, as you've got so good at this... Go deeper still... So, open your eyes... And... Close them down... Way down... Even deeper... That's good.

"In a moment, I'm going to lift your right arm and just drop it, down into your lap. Don't help me lift that arm... And when it drops down, just notice how much more, your body can relax... [arm drop] very easily... Way down...

"Now that we've reached a workable level of physical relaxation... let's continue to relax the mind too. After all, that's why we're here. So, in a moment I'm going to ask you to slowly count out loud, backwards, starting with the number 100, like this...

[Saying numbers each time the client breathes out...] "100... 99... 98...

"And after each number, just double your mental relaxation. And if you do this, you'll discover that by the time you get to 97 or even 98 you'll have relaxed your mind so beautifully and so completely, you've actually relaxed all the rest of the numbers out. Want that... And you can have it.

"So, slowly begin counting out loud, backwards, starting with the number 100, now."

Client: "100"

H: "Deeper relaxed."

C: "99"

H: "Double that relaxation."

C: "98"

H: "Now you can let those numbers grow dim and distant. They're not important."

C: "97"

H: "Now relax them right out of your mind."

C: [Client remains silent.]

H: "...All gone?"

C: "...Yeah..."

EXERCISE

Practice the Elman induction with a friend or family member. Your aim is not to achieve fluent proficiency at this stage, but to grow increasingly familiar with the process, such that it feels natural.

Some people are nervous about working with friends or family members, feeling that they can be more difficult to hypnotise. This may or may not be the case, but you would do well to pretend that it is not!

It is not necessary for your practice-partner to feel that you are a powerful hypnotist. As you progress through the process – particularly if you start with the relatively fail-proof Priority of Thought – your partner will discover that it is the process itself which is powerful. Or, perhaps, the real power resides in their mind and you are simply introducing them to a tool for tapping into that.

GRAHAM OLD

Deepening Naturally

The idea of a 'deepener' is to take someone into a deeper state of trance or deeper level of hypnosis. The understanding is often that an induction initially achieves hypnosis and that a deepener is then used to get to a sufficient level of hypnosis to give effective suggestions.

However, our understanding of inductions and of hypnosis in general is slightly different. In *The Anatomy of Inductions,* I argue that an induction is best viewed as an essential part of a fluid therapeutic process. Therefore, I am less inclined to think about levels of hypnosis that one must get down to before the real work can begin. Instead, I see hypnosis as a reframing process that enables someone to experience a shift in their perception of the world and their relationship to it.

Nevertheless, this does not mean that the concept of deepeners is completely useless to me. Precisely because I advocate a process model of hypnosis, the deepening that occurs within the Elman Induction fits nicely. Within the Elman Induction, I view the deepener as functioning to continue the process and enhance the client's current experience. This may feel like a pedantic difference, but I believe it is helpful to move us beyond a static and staggered approach into a more fluid and dynamic one.

Brief Natural Deepening

The deepener employed at this stage of the process is best framed as a brief, natural one. This is because our client has just begun to bypass their critical faculty and we want to allow that to easily and seamlessly develop into selective thinking. We do not want to allow too much time to pass between this stage and the next, as doing so may encourage unnecessary introspection and evaluation.

The fractionation that follows this stage may feel abrupt, thereby potentially jolting the client out of their experience, halting the hypnotic process. Therefore, the deepening at this stage enables things to progress just a step further and works as a useful bridge between the eye closure and the fractionation.

When Elman first taught his process, he intended for all of his students to be able to reach somnambulism in 3 minutes. He then later adjusted this to be 60 seconds. That means that there is no time for prolonged deepeners. Things are intended to move at a steady pace, progressively building on the clients experience from eye-closure all the way to the deepest 'level' of hypnosis.

There are a number of quick and easy deepeners that can be employed at this stage. Very often, following the catalepsy of the eye-lids, a hypnotist may say:

> "Okay, now, stop testing and allow that same level of relaxation to move all the way from the top of your head to the tips of your toes."

Or you may choose to utilise outside sounds and distractions:

"And any sounds that you hear will only serve to remind you what a natural process this is, allowing you to sink deeper into that experience."

Finally, you might choose to use the client's current experience as a self-perpetuating deepener:

"And as you stop testing those eye-lids, you can relax and feel great. And the better you feel, the deeper you'll go. And the deeper you go, the better you feel."

Or:

"And every breath that you take, and every word that I say and every beat of your heart will cause you to go deeper and deeper into that state."

EXERCISE

Continue to practice using the Elman induction with a friend.

Write your own versions of the deepeners included in this chapter and get feedback as to which are the most useful.

A Permissive Transcript

The following transcript is an example of the Induction that utilises permissive language, emphasising the power of the client's mind, rather than the prestige of the Hypnotist.

Hypnotist: "When you're ready, you might want to just go ahead and take a nice deep breath, fill up your lungs real good and hold it for a second. And as you breathe out... let your eyes close... And let yourself relax. That surface tension in your body can melt away, letting your shoulders relax. And let yourself go.

"I would like you to learn today just how powerful your mind really is. So, I wonder if you can imagine that every muscle around your eyelids is comfortable and getting more and more relaxed. You really can relax those eyelids as much as you want to.

"And maybe you can even imagine that those eyelids are so relaxed and so heavy that they want to stay comfortably shut. And I wonder how long it will be before you know that your imagination is so powerful that when you try in vain to open your eyes, your mind and body have accepted the suggestion that they are just too relaxed to open. And when you know that you eyes are so shut that they want to stay shut, you might even want to attempt to open them, just to prove that to yourself...

"Now, that you've proved that to yourself, you can just relax and allow that same level of relaxation to move all the way from the top of your head to the tips of your toes. And you may or may not notice, just how great that feels. And the better you feel, the deeper you can sink into that relaxation. And the deeper you go, the better you can feel.

"And any sounds that you hear can simply serve to remind you what a natural process this is, allowing you to sink deeper into that experience.

"Now let's really deepen this. In a moment, I'll invite you to open and close your eyes. When you close your eyes, you can go ahead and send a wave of relaxation through your body, so very quickly, you'll allow yourself to relax...ten times deeper. Just want it and you can have it. So, open your eyes... Now let your eyes close... And really... Let go. Feel your body relax, much more. You're doing great.

"In a moment, I'll ask you to open and close your eyes again. This time when you close your eyes, you might choose to double this physical relaxation... Really let it grow twice as deep. So, open your eyes... And close... Way down... Deeper... Deeper... Relaxed.

"In a moment, we'll do this one more time... And notice how easily it occurs this time as you learn how simple it is... Going even deeper. All right, open your eyes... And... Way down... really let go. That's good.

"And in a moment, I'm going to lift your right arm and drop it. And, because you have relaxed so well, you can find that your arm will be heavy and relaxed. And when it drops down, just notice how much more, your body can drop down deeply into that state. Very easily. [Lifts Arm] Don't help me lift it. That's it. [Drops arm] ...Perfect. Way down. Great...

"Now that you have achieved physical relaxation, let's go on to relax your mind as well. And, in fact, physical relaxation is by far the more difficult for most people to reach and you have already shown that you can do that easily. So, let me teach you how to relax your mind, with some very simple steps. In a moment, I will invite you to begin to spell your name backwards, starting at the end of your surname. Like this...

"A... [wait for next exhalation]... N... And so on. And you can double that relaxation with each letter. And what you will find is that within just a few letters, you will have reached such a calm serene state that those letters will just melt away.

"All you have to do is want it and you can make it happen; you can easily relax your mind in this way. So, go ahead now and *begin* to spell your name backwards, doubling your relaxation with each letter."

Client: "A"

H: "Doubling that relaxation..."

C: "N"

H: "Letters fading away..."

C: "I"

H: "Deeper relaxed..."

C: [Silence]

H: "Letters all gone?"

C: "Yeah."

EXERCISE

Keep practising the Elman induction with friends and family members.

Do you feel more comfortable with a permissive or authoritarian style? Practice with the approach that you are initially less comfortable with.

Get feedback from your practice partner, as to which style connected with them most effectively.

If you are able to, have someone practice the Elman induction with you as the client. Does your preferred style for practising the induction match your preferred style when you are on the receiving end?

Fractionation

Dave Elman called the stage of Fractionation, "Three trips to Bernheim." This is because Elman first encountered this principle in Hippolyte Bernheim's classic text, 'Suggestive Therapeutics'.

The Theory

Bernheim discovered that the more that patients came to see him, the deeper they would go into hypnosis. He states that when patients came in for their fifth session they went into a much deeper state of hypnosis. Elman reasoned that if the patients returned for five days in a row (rather than five weeks), they would reach this deep state more quickly. Then he thought that the visits could be just an hour apart. Finally, he discovered that this could all be experienced within one session, allowing Elman to achieve in three minutes what it took Bernheim five weeks to do.

This is the reason that the induction that we call the Elman Induction was referred to as 'the repeated inductions technique' by Elman himself.

The process of repeatedly taking someone into and out of hypnosis has acquired the label, *Fractionation*. It functions as an additional natural deepener and is disarmingly powerful. Additionally, the speed with which such fractionation takes place within the Elman Induction serves to convince the client that this process is indeed working, further cementing the bypass of the critical faculty and ensuring selective thinking. In short, they believe that you know what you are doing, that what you are doing works and that they are experiencing the result.

Here are the three trips to Bernheim at their most simple:

> Hypnotist: "Now let's really deepen this experience for you. In a moment, I'll ask you to open your eyes and then close them. When you close your eyes, send a wave of relaxation through your body and go 10 times deeper into this state. Just want it and you can have it. So, go ahead and open your eyes..."
>
> Client: [Opens eyes.]
>
> H: "And... [Waits until client is about to exhale]... close your eyes... and go ten times deeper. That's it.
>
> "In a moment, I'll ask you to open and close your eyes again. This time when you close your eyes, you can double this physical relaxation... Going twice as deep. So, open your eyes..."
>
> C: [Opens eyes.]
>
> H: "And... [Waits until client is about to exhale]... close your eyes... and go twice as

deep. That's perfect.

"So, let's do that one more time. Next time I ask you to open your eyes and close them you will go deeper still, just let go and go as deep as you can. So, go ahead and open your eyes..."

C: [Opens eyes.]

H: "And... [Waits until client is about to exhale]... close your eyes... All the way down. Deeper and deeper."

We have written elsewhere about the value of fractionation.[22] It is difficult to think of a single induction or hypnotic process that it cannot be usefully incorporated into. For now, let us explore a couple of points that it may be beneficial to be aware of, as far as fractionation relates to the Elman Induction.

The Practice

Many practitioners of the Elman Induction recommend placing your hand a few inches in front of the patient's eyes as they open them. As they open their eyes and see your hand, you can then raise it ever so slightly and they will naturally follow your hand up. Then, lower it down again as you instruct them to close their eyes. The idea is to prevent them from focusing on something else, or

---

22 See Old, (2014). *Mastering the Leisure Induction*.

being distracted in some way. Personally, I find this to be completely unnecessary.

The very idea of fractionation is for your client to come out of hypnosis and go back in. If I am really confident in the process, then I have no reason to fear them focusing on something, being distracted in some way, or coming completely out of hypnosis. The only reason that would be a concern is if it was particularly important to me that the client did not come out of hypnosis and merely opened and closed their eyes.

However, Elman was clear that he viewed the suggestions to go ten times deeper, twice as deep and deeper still as post-hypnotic suggestions. And post-hypnotic suggestions require someone to come out of hypnosis before they can go back in. For that reason, I do not place my hand in front of their eyes.

Having said that, I do not let too much time pass between them opening their eyes and closing them again. So, I doubt they really have time to get focused on things around them. Ordinarily, I have them close their eyes the next time they breathe out. This is a natural time for them to close their eyes, aids relaxation and maintains the pace of the induction.

Another reason why you might not want to put your hand in front of their eyes relates to Elman's five signs of hypnosis. I want to be able to get a good look at their eyes, to note any reddening or watering of the eyes. If my hand is up in front of their face, this can potentially block my view and deny me a valuable piece of information.

Some of the patter used at this point in the process may seem slightly arbitrary. After all, if I am not sold on the idea of depths of hypnosis, why do I talk about going ten times deeper? And, if I do hold to that model, why would I not suggest going 100 times deeper instead? Larry Elman addresses this question well:

> When you begin fractionation, the subject is capable of visualising 10 times deeper, so the suggestion "takes." You have no idea where the subject *thinks* he is, so on the second pass you use twice as deep – always an attainable goal because it is within the subject's perception. By the third pass you have *even less of an idea of where the subject thinks he is, or how deep he thinks he can go*, and since you do not want a rejection of a suggestion tied to a particular number, you say "deeper yet." ...Experiment with this one and you will find that "10 times; twice as deep; deeper still" is a good formula for most clients.[23]

This seems like good advice to me. I have seen some hypnotists using such hyperbolic language as "a million times deeper" and so on. Not only is that difficult for most of us to imagine, but it risks bringing the whole process in to ridicule.

---

23 Elman, H.L, (2011), pp. 26-27.

EXERCISE

Fractionation is a powerful and widely used tool by contemporary hypnotists. What is your explanation for why it is so beneficial?

Can you think of ways to employ fractionation, that are more subtle than having your client open and close their eyes?

Continue to practice the Elman induction. Experiment with the fractionation stage, both with using your hand in front of their eyes and also with more subtle or conversational examples.

Get feedback from your practice partner(s) as to which felt more effective.

Magnetic Fingers Transcript

The following transcript employs magnetic fingers, rather than the eye-lock, as the initial catalepsy. If you pay attention to the fractionation, you will see that it also uses progressively direct language, an idea taken from the PHRIT process.[24]

Hypnotist: "Well, to start us off, just get yourself comfortable..."

Client: [Shifts slightly in their chair]

H: "And if at any point, you want to move around and get even more comfortable, that's just fine.

"Okay, what I'd like you to do now... I'd like you to place your hands out in front of you, like this..." [Demonstrates by holding his hands out in front, palms touching.]

H: "And now interlock your fingers and bend

---

24 See http://www.howtodoinductions.com/inductions/phrit and Old, G. (2016). *Revisiting Hypnosis*. Milton Keynes: 61 Books.

your elbows up like this ...as if you're praying, or begging for your life!" [laughs]

C: [Client copies exactly]

H: "That's it... Clasp your hands together, palms touching, so you can feel them touching, nice and tight.

"Now, in a moment, I'll ask you to extend your fore-fingers and point towards the ceiling. And when you do that, I'll click my fingers which will be a signal to your subconscious mind to magnetise those fingertips. Ready?"

C: [Smiles.] "Yep."

H: "Okay, now, point your fingers up. Separate them, about an inch or so, point right up."

H: [Clicks fingers]

H: "And now watch your fingertips, focus on the space between them, magnetised... pulling... closer and closer. Just like they're magnets."

C: [Fingers come together in a matter of seconds.]

H: "Now, as they touch, you can imagine them being so strongly joined that it is as if they have melted into one big finger. Just imagine that. Allow that idea to wrap around that finger there, wrapping tighter and tighter. You can feel it magnetised, joined, melded in the middle and you might even have begun to notice them being squeezed together from the outside. And when you know that they are completely joined together, so joined together that you could not part them without unwrapping that idea, go ahead and try to pull them apart and notice them joining even tighter...."

C: [Client's elbows move as they try to part their fingers, but they remain together.]

H: "Wow. You've got a powerful mind. Now, you can stop trying and just relax. Allow your eyes to close and relax. And your hands can float down gently to your lap... Parting as they do. That's it. Resting on your lap... And as you breath out... just relax.

"You've got a great imagination. So, what I want you to do now is just take a long deep breath, fill up your lungs real good and hold it for a second. Now as you exhale, just send a wave of relaxation all the way down your body..."

C: [Breathes out deeply]

H: "That's it... All the way down... to the tips of your toes.

"And, in fact, every time you breathe out, you can go deeper and deeper into that relaxation.

"Now let's deepen this experience even further. Every breath that you take, every word that I say and every beat of your heart, will allow you to sink deeper and deeper into that pleasant relaxation.

"In a moment, I'm going to ask you to open your eyes and then close them. When you close your eyes, send a wave of relaxation through your body and go ten times deeper into this state. Just want it and you can have it. So, go ahead and open your eyes..."

Client: [Opens eyes.]

H: "And... [Waits until client is about to exhale]... close your eyes... and go ten times deeper. That's it.

"In a moment, I'll ask you to open and close your eyes again. This time when you close your eyes, you can double this physical relaxation... Letting go and going twice as deep. So, open your eyes..."

C: [Opens eyes.]

H: "And... [Waits until client is about to exhale]... close your eyes... going twice as deep. That's perfect.

"So, let's do that one more time. Next time I ask you to open your eyes and close them you will go deeper still, you'll go as deep as you can. So, go ahead and open your eyes..."

C: [Opens eyes.]

H: "And... [Waits until client is about to exhale]... close your eyes... All the way down. Deeper and deeper.

"And in a moment, I'm going to lift your right arm and drop it. Don't help me lift that arm... And when it drops down, just notice how much deeper you can go. "

H: [Lifts arm up, swings it slightly from left to right. Then drops it onto the client's leg.]

H: "All the way down. That's it.

"Now we want your body to be as relaxed as

your mind. So, in a moment I'm going to ask you to count out slowly like this..."

H: [Saying numbers each time the client breathes out...] "100... 99... 98...

"And after each number, double your mental relaxation. And if you do this, you'll discover that by the time you get to 97 or even 98 you'll have relaxed all of those numbers out of your mind. Want that... And you can have it.

"So, slowly begin counting out loud, backwards, starting with the number 100, now."

C: "100"

H: "And double that relaxation."

C: "99"

H: "That's it. Deeper and deeper."

C: "98"

H: "Now relax them right out of your mind."

C: "97"

THE ELMAN INDUCTION

H: "Push them away."

C: [Client remains silent.]

H: "All gone?"

C: "Yes."

H: "That's great."

EXERCISE

Keep practising the Elman induction.

The various transcripts throughout this book provide a mixture of authoritarian approaches and permissive ones, empowering and therapeutic. Begin to practice using these and other approaches.

Try replacing some parts of the process with alternatives. Instead of the eye-lock, try using magnetic fingers.

What other examples of the initial catalepsy could you employ?

Experiment. Get feedback. Adjust what you are doing. Then experiment some more!

The Arm-Drop

The next stage is more properly entitled, *Catalepsy of a Group of Large Muscles*. However, it is more commonly described as an arm-drop. Medical definitions differ in seeing catalepsy as solely referring to a rigidity of muscles, or seeing it as an extreme of *either* rigidity or looseness. Elman viewed it as the latter, a loss of muscle control, so this stage can involve either a floppy arm-drop or a stiff-arm.

In Elman's mind, the arm catalepsy serves a number of purposes:

Indicator

The catalepsy signals to you that your client is following your suggestions and also convinces them that the suggestions are effective. It demonstrates that things are progressing as planned. However, it is more than that.

With both the stiff-arm and the arm-drop, you do not merely see how stiff or heavy the arm is; you suggest it. This stage then is all about achieving catalepsy *by suggestion*.

Deepener

By further demonstrating to your client that the process is indeed working, it secures their engagement and deepens the experience. However, both the stiff-arm and the arm-drop contain a kinaesthetic element that takes the deepening to another level.

If you use the stiff-arm, the idea is not to leave the client in that position. After all, that does nothing to aid their relaxation, which I will later argue is an essential element of the induction. Here is Elman describing this variation:

> Elman: [to hypnotized patient] Close your eyes; just pretend you can't open them. I'm going to take your arm and I want you to extend it and make it rigid as I count to three. Make that so rigid you can't bend it. One – make it rigid – two, like steel – three, now you can't bend it no matter how hard you try. When you try, it just won't work at all. Test it. You'll find you can't bend it at all.

However, he continues:

> Elman: [to patient] Now when I have you relax the arm, you'll go much deeper... Now you can relax. Relax and you'll go much deeper...[25]

If I use the stiff-arm during the Elman process, I then shake the arm by the wrist and say something like, "And now, relax, instantly" before dropping the arm in to their

25 Elman, (1977) pp. 47-48.

lap. So, both variations include the element of dropping the arm, which is a powerful physical expression of relaxation. The resultant drop signifies to the client how you want them to be feeling.

Hypnosis as a form of relaxation?

I would like to make an argument at this point which may be uncommon, but is straight from Elman himself: The form of hypnosis sought in the Elman Induction is a form of relaxation.

I do not mean to say that Elman thought that Hypnosis and relaxation were identical. He points out in a number of places that if you do not get selective thinking then you do not have hypnosis; you merely have relaxation. However, he was also very clear in stating:

'Hypnosis is a form of relaxation.'[26]

In fact, when referring to somnambulism – a topic to which we shall return – Elman argued that, 'When the patient is mentally relaxed as well as physically relaxed, we have somnambulism.'[27]

A number of years ago, I was discussing the Elman Induction with Larry Elman and I suggested that the induction is a thinly disguised version of a progressive relaxation induction. Larry disagreed and no doubt believed I had not fully understood his father's work. However, I stand by my claim, as I believe it is a claim made by Dave Elman himself.

You know already that hypnosis is a form of

---

26 ibid., p. 114.
27 ibid., p. 95.

relaxation. As the patient relaxes more and more, deeper and deeper, a feeling of euphoria is brought on – a feeling of well-being, of contentment – which the patient has perhaps never before known. As this feeling increases, he gets a greater sense of confidence in himself and the doctor. In this euphoric state it seems to the patient that all is right with the world and that anything within human reason is possible. He therefore accepts at face value – without criticism – any suggestion that appears reasonable and pleasing to him.[28]

This may be a unique kind of relaxation that is being described, but it is relaxation nonetheless. It is rapid progressive relaxation (physical and mental), coupled with a bypass of the critical faculty, leading to selective thinking and the suspension of disbelief. The fact that the Elman Induction enables us to do all of this within three minutes (or even 60 seconds) is a remarkable thing.

Why do I bring this up now? It is to drive home the point that at any stage within the Elman Induction almost anything you do has a dual purpose. At any one time, you are seeking to increase relaxation *and* secure selective thinking. At other times, you will be providing a convincer for the client, whilst also deepening their experience. Similarly, at some points you are testing where the client is, whilst simultaneously taking them deeper. The arm drop is an excellent example of all of these.

If I was a hypnotee, unsure that the induction was working on me, the arm-drop would be a strong sign that it was. Not only would it demonstrate that I had relaxed

_____
28 ibid., pp. 114-115.

my whole body incredibly quickly, but it would appear that I had done that in response to the hypnotist's suggestion. Well then, that could only mean that they were a competent hypnotist and this was an effective process! Yet, even more than that, the physical feeling of going deeper into hypnosis would be reinforced to me with a solid plop of my heavy arm on to my lap.

On top of all of that, I would have just demonstrated to the hypnotist that I was exactly where I needed to be – and ready for somnambulism.

EXERCISE

What do you make of Elman's statement that 'Hypnosis is a form of relaxation'?

In what ways is this helpful? And in what ways is it not?

Find someone new to practice the induction with, but do not use the word 'hypnosis'. Instead you might speak of "rapid relaxation" or something similar.

Note any advantages or disadvantages to this terminology and any ways that the induction feels different to usual, when carried out under this description.

Stiff-Arm Transcript

The following transcript begins with a catalepsy of the little finger, instead of eye-closure. It then builds on that idea by using stiff-arm catalepsy instead of a limp or floppy arm drop.

Hypnotist: "Why don't you start by just taking a nice long deep breath... And let's just do a couple more of them... maybe each time you breathe-in... [waits for inhalation]

"...it's as if you're breathing in peace and calm... And each time you breathe-out... [waits for exhalation]

"...just letting go of any stress and tension... That's excellent."

Client: [Moves shoulders around, as if looking for a comfortable position.]

H: "And, yeah, you can go right ahead and just find a comfortable position. And if at any point you want to get more comfortable, that's fine too."

C: [Sighs and closes eyes.]

H: "Woh... No, not yet. Open your eyes a minute."

C: [Opens eyes.]

H: "Gee, you're eager, aren't you?!" [Laughs]

C: [Laughs]

H: "Well, look, what I want you to do, before you can really let go and close your eyes... I'd like you just to look down at your hand there on your thigh. And just notice your little finger. I wonder what it's like to be that little finger there so relaxed?

"What I'd like you to do for me now is allow all strength and tension to leave that hand, exiting through the finger. That's it. Relax that hand completely and allow all tension and stress and strength and energy to come out through that finger...

"And when you know that the finger has relaxed enough... that all tension has gone... when you know that you've relaxed that finger so much that you couldn't lift that finger without putting tension back in, go ahead and try to lift it and find that it's just too relaxed to move..."

C: [Client's shoulder moves slightly and they smile as they cannot lift their little finger.]

H: "Okay, now you can stop trying... And close your eyes... And let that same relaxation float all the way to the top of your head... and sink all the way down to your toes.

"Let go of every muscle. Let go of every nerve. Let go of every fibre... And let yourself drift much, deeper, relaxed... Perfect.

"Now let's really deepen this. In a moment, I'll ask you to open your eyes and close them again. And when you close your eyes, you can send a wave of relaxation through your body, that will allow you to relax 10 times deeper.

"So, open your eyes... And close... going 10 times deeper.

"In a moment, I'll ask you to open and close your eyes again. This time when you close your eyes, you can double this physical relaxation... Going twice as deep.

"So, open your eyes... And close them again... Twice as deep.

"And once more... This time, we'll have you open your eyes and when you close them you'll go deep down, deeper still. So, open your eyes... And close them again... That's it... all the way down.

"Now, in a moment, I will take your arm, lifting it up by the wrist. And I want you to extend that arm out, stiff as an iron rod."

H: [Takes up arm, which is already stiff and rigid.]

"That's it. Make a fist." [Taps end of fist.]

"Solid. ...as if there is iron through the middle and steel wrapped around it. Unbendable. Just go ahead and try and bend that arm and find that it just won't bend."

C: [Arm shakes as client tries to bend it, but does not bend.]

H: "Now you can stop trying... And as I shake the arm like this [shaking arm by the wrist] it just becomes limp and loose and relaxed, like a wet dishcloth... That's it.

"And as I drop your arm into your lap, you can just go even deeper... [drops arm] ...all the way

94

down."

C: [Client's arm lands heavily on their thigh, as their head drops forward.]

H: "Well, we now want your mind to enjoy the same level of relaxation that your body is. So, in a moment, I'm going to ask you to slowly begin counting out loud, backwards, starting with the number 100. After each number, double your mental relaxation. Now if you do this, you'll discover that by the time you get to 97 or 96, you will have relaxed the numbers right out of your mind. Want that... And you can have it.

"So, now, slowly begin counting out loud, backwards, starting with the number 100."

C: "100"

H: "Double that relaxation."

C: "99"

H: "Deeper relaxed now."

C: "98"

H: "Just let those numbers fade away."

C: "97"

H: "Deeper relaxed... fading away."

C: "96"

H: "Now push them on out, just tell them to leave and they will go. Just let them go... And let them be gone."

C: [Silence]

H: "...All gone?"

C: "Yes."

EXERCISE

By now, you should be familiar with the induction and with the way that its various parts can be substituted, as long as the process is followed.

As you continue to practice, simply note which version(s) of the induction feels most natural to you. That is, which one fits your overall approach, your style, manner and model of hypnosis?

Consider whether it is better to focus primarily on the version which is most natural to you (thereby improving and specialising your skills), or whether you and your clients are best served by continuing to experiment with different alternatives.

GRAHAM OLD

The Compounding of Suggestions

'This is the thing that makes Hypnosis work. From the beginning of hypnosis to its deepest state, it is all a matter of compounding. All you're doing at all times is developing a better state – a greater depth.' (Dave Elman)[29]

We come now to an aspect of the Elman induction that is so pervasive throughout the whole process that it would be possible to miss its unique importance. To a degree, the compounding of suggestions might be seen as an extension of the fractionation stage of the induction. In reality, the fractionation is merely one example of an element that is at the very core of the process.

Compounding suggestions refers to the practice of repeating, restating, reinforcing and re-experiencing suggestions. As said, it can take the form of fractionation, whereby repeatedly suggesting and practising going into hypnosis increases its effect. However, it can be used to reinforce any number of suggestions.

To be clear, compounding suggestions is not exactly the same as simply repeating a suggestion a dozen or so times. Understood in an Elmanian sense, compounding is making a suggestion and having the patient follow and experience the effects of the suggestion, then making the

29 ibid., p. 108.

suggestion again and so on. It is not merely the repetition of suggestions, but the re-experience of suggestions being given and carried out effectively that is the essence of compounding.

Elman demonstrates the effect of compounding on suggestions for anaesthesia:

> Elman: Now, I will stroke your right hand, and watch the anaesthesia come in. Your hand is going to get so numb. I'll stroke it three times. One...two...three... How's your hand?

> Patient: It feels cold.

> Elman: All right, that means the anaesthesia is starting. When I have you open your eyes, that anaesthesia is going to get ten times as strong... Open your eyes... How is your hand now?

> Patient: It feels funny.

> Elman: [to doctors] ...If we want to have that anaesthesia get stronger we can have her do almost anything and any act she goes through – any suggestion she follows – will make that anaesthesia stronger. For example [to patient] raise your left hand and drop it... What happened to your right hand when you did that?

> Patient: It feels funnier?

Elman: Funnier than before, is that right?

Patient: Yes.[30]

As you can see, Elman is not simply repeating the suggestion for anaesthesia. Instead, he is making the suggestion that any action that is carried out will increase the anaesthesia – and he then has his patient carry out a number of actions to experience this.

The same effect could have been achieved if Elman had said that each time he touched their hand it would get more and more numb. Or he could have simply described the anaesthesia in increasingly detailed ways, having his patient experience the increase with each description.

Here is how Gerald Kein, a student of Elman's, describes the compounding of suggestions:

'When you give the first suggestion of change to the client, it's very weak. It is so weak, it will have little to no effect. The second suggestion makes the first suggestion stronger but then the second suggestion is weak. The third suggestion reinforces and makes stronger the first suggestion and then it makes stronger the second suggestion, but it itself is weak. As you give the client suggestions, the first, second, third etc. always get stronger. It always goes back to the first suggestion and makes it and the succeeding suggestions

---

30 ibid., p. 100.

stronger.'[31]

Within this practice, we are getting a glimpse of a kernel of truth that may demonstrate just why the Elman Induction is so effective. As each suggestion is given, it reiterates and reinforces the previous suggestions. This can be the case with identical suggestions that are strengthened, for example, increasing anaesthesia. Yet, it can also be the case with related suggestions, such as those for physical and then mental relaxation.

It is this latter example that demonstrates why the compounding of suggestions is such an important concept for appreciating the power of the Elman Induction.

The Process of Consent

We have already discussed the place of consent within the Elman induction. However, it is helpful to think of consent, not as a one-off decision, but as an ongoing state of mind. This would seem to be why Elman refers to hypnosis itself as a 'state of consent', rather than merely the result of consent given at the beginning of the process.[32]

If we were to take a step back and look at the client's experience of the induction, from beginning to end, we might see something like this:

---

31 Kein, Gerald, The Law Of Hypnotic Compounding, http://hypnothoughts.com/gerald-kein/blog/408/the-law-of-hypnotic-compounding
32 The word 'state' is being used rather loosely here. I will examine the terminology more closely when we look at the topic of somnambulism below.

- A suggestion for relaxation of the eyelids is given and experienced as catalepsy
- This involves – and increases – the idea that the hypnotist is somehow directing their experience of reality (that is, they experience a bypassing of their critical faculty)
- Suggestion for increased relaxation is given and experienced
- Repeated opening and closing of the eyes increases this relaxation even more
- Client becomes increasingly aware of the fact that they are experiencing precisely what the hypnotist suggests
- Catalepsy of the arm is experienced, followed by an arm-drop that evidences and increases relaxation
- Amnesia is suggested and experienced

That is a fairly accurate description of how things are often experienced by the client. From a hypnotist's perspective, we might notice 3 ongoing processes taking place at the same time, each influencing the others:

1. Consent and Following Suggestions
2. Bypassing the critical faculty (including and leading to selective thinking)
3. Physical and Mental Relaxation

Each of these processes increases in effect as the induction continues. Each suggestion that is given builds upon and strengthens the previous suggestions. This is more than simply compounding suggestions and perhaps is best described as *Cascading Suggestions*.

Compounding suggestions usually refers to the same

suggestion given and experienced a number of times. The idea is sometimes stretched to include related ideas. For example, physical relaxation may be connected to mental calm which may be connected to physical heaviness which can be associated with mental absorption and so on. Depending on your model of psychology, you might think that the same 'state' is being suggested and this is why clients allow the suggestions to impact each other in that way. I tend to view it more as a result of associations and connections, which would seem to play a large role in how our minds make sense of experiences.

Nevertheless, compounding is taken to refer to the same, similar or related suggestions given and followed more than once. Cascading suggestions builds upon this idea.

Pyramiding Suggestions

When it comes to suggestions for hypnotic phenomena, whether that is a hand stuck to a leg, or a needle inserted painlessly into an arm, a useful idea that some people subscribe to is the notion of 'pyramiding suggestions'. The idea is that someone may easily experience something like magnetic hands, so you start there.[33] When they have achieved that – which it is difficult not to do, unless they are intentionally resisting you – you then build on it by sticking their hands together. Once you have that, you could stick their hand to their head and so on. Or you might start with an unbendable arm and gradually build on up to analgesia in the arm.

It is a simple idea and not without merit. In one sense,

---

33 See, for example,
http://www.howtodoinductions.com/exercises/magnetic

this is an example of experiential pacing and leading. You take what you and the client know they can experience and lead from there on to the next. At no point are you taking yourself too far out of your comfort zone, or pushing them beyond what they might perceive to be possible. As what they experience increases, the notion of what is or is not possible also grows. You then build up and up until you reach the point you are aiming for.

This is a useful concept, which is easily grasped. However, I prefer to take a slightly different approach.

Cascading Suggestions

Personally, I find it more beneficial to think of moving *down* the pyramid, not up. This is true not just in the case of phenomena, but – as we see with the Elman Induction – with the hypnotic process itself.

Think of the first brick at the very top of the pyramid as your first suggestion. "You might want to just go ahead and close your eyes", for example. This suggestion is easily followed and that action in itself makes your client more likely to follow the next. As your suggestions increase – as you move 'deeper' down the pyramid – the number of bricks increases also. As I envisage the model, this refers to the number of potential suggestions – with an increasing number of connections and associations – that can be made.

Consider this for a moment, as I refer back to the 3 processes at work throughout the entire Elman Induction:

1. Consent and Following Suggestions
2. Bypassing the critical faculty (including and leading to selective thinking)

3. Physical and Mental Relaxation

At the beginning of the induction, the client may not consent to much more than sitting where you ask, answering questions that are not too intrusive and possibly closing their eyes. Having closed their eyes, they relax and this relaxation leads them to accept the suggestion that their eyes will not open. They experience this catalepsy, which leads them to giving more credibility to both you and the process. Suggestions are given for rapid relaxation, which is experienced successfully. As each suggestion is accepted, the degree of consent and credibility which the client affords you, allows for an increasing number of phenomena to be experienced. Almost simultaneously, consent, selective thinking and physical and mental relaxation cascade all of the way down to amnesia and deeper.

It is not necessary to conclude from this model that I am suggesting that a certain 'depth' of hypnosis needs to be reached before some phenomena can be achieved. Although that is a popular notion, research does not currently appear to support it. A good number of people seem able to achieve all manner of hypnotic phenomena – including anaesthesia or visual/auditory hallucinations – at any of the supposed 'levels' of hypnosis.[34]

However, what this model does demonstrate is that some clients may benefit by being eased into the experience. As they proceed, their belief in what is possible – and therefore the consent they will give and credibility they will perceive – increases. The number of

34 Cf. Wood & Barnier. 2008. Hypnosis Scales for the twenty-first century: what do we need and how should we use them? In: Nash & Barnier ed. *The Oxford Handbook of Hypnosis*. Oxford: OUP, pp. 3-15.

suggestions that will be accepted and by implication the variety of effects that will be achievable increases as the process continues.

For some people, this will be experienced as moving from 'easier' to 'harder' phenomena, the deeper they go into their experience. However, in essence it is simply the fact that each suggestion that is accepted increases the likelihood of the next suggestion being followed. In actuality, it is *a cascading of consent* and relaxation which results in a growing bypass of the critical faculty and selective thinking.

Viewed in this way, it is easy to see why we initially made the argument that it is essential to view the Elman Induction as a process. It is so clearly not simply a case of repeating magic words from a script which, when performed perfectly and recited exactly, bring about hypnosis. Instead, the induction is your opportunity to take someone on a journey where they experience a progressive shift in their experience of reality.

Elman understood this differently to how we have framed things above. However, the notion of cascading suggestions fits naturally into his model. Elman perceived this induction as taking someone on a journey – where you are their 'dream pilot' – from the waking state all the way into somnambulism. It is to this topic that we now turn.

EXERCISE

On page 103, we discussed how the Elman induction is experienced by our clients. Then we looked at the three ongoing processes at work, from the hypnotist's perspective.

Re-write these sections in your own words. From *your* practice of the induction, what would you say your client experiences as the induction progresses? Better yet, ask the person that you have just practised on!

As the hypnotist, how would *you* describe the processes at work?

How useful is the idea of cascading suggestions? In your own words, clarify the difference between compounding, pyramiding and cascading suggestions.

Losing the Numbers

The next stage in the process is commonly labelled 'losing the numbers'. However, it is more accurately described as amnesia by suggestion.

Four True States of Hypnosis

Dave Elman taught that there were four 'true states of hypnosis', in addition to the waking state, which should be of interest.[35] They are:

1. Light or superficial
2. Somnambulistic
3. The Esdaile / Coma state
4. Hypnosis attached to sleep

As previously stated, the *repeated induction technique* was intended to lead someone into somnambulism within three minutes, if not just 60 seconds.

Elman believed that patients are less critical of suggestions given to them in somnambulism and suggestions 'go into his mind deeper and remain longer than in the light state.'[36] As he was working with Doctors

---

35 ibid., (1977), p. 98.
36 ibid.

and Dentists, who were relying on hypnosis to provide an effective anaesthesia, it is easy to see why Elman was so keen on ensuring his students could reliably take a patient into somnambulism.

This is not the place to argue for or against the concept of somnambulism or different levels of hypnosis. Our focus remains the practice and experience of hypnosis. Nevertheless, it may be useful to explore the concept of somnambulism in more depth, to see where it may or may not be useful and to consider ways in which it can be utilised or revamped. We will then turn to the practice of achieving amnesia by suggestion.

The State of Somnambulism

Different schools of hypnosis hold to different theories on the existence or nature of various levels of hypnosis. Some connect them to particular brain activity, whilst others view it in less literal ways. There are also different understandings of the signs that someone is at a particular level or state of hypnosis. Amongst those who believe there are different levels of hypnosis, there is also no agreement on exactly how many levels there are.

For example, the Arons Depth Scale has 6 levels of hypnosis, the Stanford Scale has 12 levels, the Davis-Husband scale has 30, whilst the LeCron-Bordeaux has 50!

We have already seen that Elman holds to a 4-level model. He sees somnambulism as the state at which you can achieve amnesia by suggestion. Beneath that is the Coma state, in which the patient is completely immobilised and anaesthesia is achieved automatically, without suggestion. We will return to this later.

THE ELMAN INDUCTION

It is worth remembering that, according to Elman, patients can still reject suggestions and rouse themselves if felt necessary, in both the coma state and somnambulism. What then is the advantage of using the Elman induction to reach somnambulism? As stated above, it is believed – by those who follow Elman – to be a level at which suggestions go deeper and last longer. The number of suggestions that will be accepted is maximised and only those likely to cause offence or appear irrational will be rejected. If Elman is correct, it is a hypnotist's dream!

From my perspective, it is neither necessary to accept or reject the notion of somnambulism. I do not think that effective use of the Elman induction requires acceptance or rejection of the concept. However, from an experiential position, it makes sense to seek to lead my clients to a place where they are likely to accept the highest number of suggestions – and to have those suggestions last for as long as possible. It matters not whether this is an actual distinct level of hypnosis, as long as it is an experience we can assist out clients to enter into. The Elman Induction, due to how it is progressively structured, is an ideal tool for enabling clients to get to a point where they can readily accept suggestions for a sustained period of time.

It may therefore be more beneficial to think of Elman's 'Four True States of Hypnosis' as four aspects of the hypnotic experience. I do not use the Elman Induction to guarantee that I can get client's to a certain state of hypnosis. I use it because it has proven to be a reliable means of taking client's through an experience which reaches a point where they can easily accept my suggestions. In my mind, it is the experience of cascaded suggestions which enables this, yet almost without fail my clients are more interested in the reality of the hypnotic experience than the theory or labels used to describe it.

Conditions, States and Moods

It would seem that we can view the Elman Induction as a process designed to takes client's on a journey. The destination is significant – the point of almost complete consent. Yet it is the process along the way which enables such a destination to be within our reach. We can think of the Elman Induction then as a teaching exercise, which practically and progressively leads clients to the 'state' of mind desired.

So it is that I believe it is possible to use the induction just as Elman intended, to achieve the exact results he spoke of, without necessarily needing to feel bound by his explanation of the theory behind what he did.

Although Elman spoke of states and apparently built his whole model around this, he does not actually occupy the same ground as many of those today described as 'state theorists'. In fact, his very understanding of the 'state' of hypnosis is more fluid than static, more phenomenological than purely theoretical.

Elman argued that hypnosis is a 'state of mind' rather than a 'condition':

> 'Now, what is the difference between a condition and a state of mind? In the first place, you are not in a hypnotic condition as you read these words. If I wanted to put you into a so-called hypnotic condition, I would have to change your present condition. Not many people are willing to have their condition

changed. A question of semantics perhaps, but an important one since the state of mind, unlike its condition, frequently and easily changes. The state of mind of hypnosis can be obtained instantaneously, for a state of mind is merely a mood, and I maintain that hypnosis is merely a mood.[37]

By describing hypnosis as a 'mood', Elman actually drifts closer to the kind of position held by leading Ericksonian scholar, Jeffrey Zeig. Elman and Zeig use contradictory language, as Zeig distinguishes between states and moods, whereas Elman above demonstrates that he uses 'state of mind' loosely to describe what others might call a mood.

Zeig presents a phenomenological model of states that fits well with our experiential focus and fits comfortably alongside Elman's model. In *The Induction of Hypnosis*, Zeig distinguishes between three aspects of human experience: emotions, moods and states. Emotions are fleeting visceral experiences, such as sadness, disgust, anger or fear. Moods, by contrast, are more stable over time and can be experienced over sustained periods of time. Zeig notes that when patients seek therapy it is often because they feel trapped within a negative mood and unable to change it.

States, as Zeig describes them, are a complex of interactions, emotions, memories, moods, attitudes, beliefs and habits.

> "States" are "syndromes", not entities... They are "titles" for groupings of experiences. "States" are constructs of convenience that

---

37 ibid., p. 26.

allow people to conveniently communicate their immediate experience.

...."States" are subjective realities that we know from common experience. "States" also are phenomenological realities that are part of lived experience; they are not constant in that they change over time as circumstances alter.[38]

Within Zeig's model, examples of states include: Open-minded, lazy, focused, unkind, resilient, inhibited, positive, doubting and engaged.

It can be seen that although Zeig distinguishes between moods and states – whereas Elman sees the state of hypnosis as a mood – they are both using the concept of a 'state of mind' in similar ways. It describes a number of elements that make up the clients experience, including the inter-personal aspect between the hypnotist and client.

If the reader will allow me one more quote from Zeig, it can be seen how hypnosis and the concept of states may be useful partners:

'When the patient comes for therapy, it is as if the patient is in reverse, suffering limitations in interaction, mobility, and perception. The application of a successful induction moves the patient into a neutral "state", and out of the calcified, problem "state". The application of a successful induction can be a reference experience that demonstrates to the patient that he can change his "state". Sometimes movement into "neutral" hypnosis itself can be

---

38 The Induction of Hypnosis, pp. 30-33.

a systematically significant intervention; the momentum engendered by changing "states" can initiate momentum in the patient to move forward and change or cope adequately.'[39]

Aside from echoing aspects of our argument in *The Anatomy of Inductions*, Zeig helpfully demonstrates a productive way to employ the concept of states within the Elman process. It may be that we are not simply moving a client to a 'state' of hypnosis where they will respond to the highest number of suggestions, but that we are piloting them to a state of mind that is resourceful, adaptable and teachable. In fact, the entire process becomes one of experiential learning that guarantees the cascading of suggestion-response and enables the client to reach a point where they share with you the experience of shaping a new reality.

Amnesia by Suggestion

Elman's reasoning for why somnambulism allows amnesia by suggestion is enticing. He argues that it involves a state of mind that is so euphoric that it accepts uncritically any suggestion that appears reasonable and pleasing to the client.[40]

This certainly seems to match the experience of clients that I have spoken to. Rather than describing reaching a state where they were robotically responding to any and every suggestion, they tend to speak of a state of mind that is so content that it does not think to resist

---

39 ibid., p. 39.
40 Elman, (1977), pp. 114-115.

suggestions that are not inherently objectionable to them. This is not so much an experience of hyper-suggestibility as it is an experience of contented consent. And, as Elman says, 'when there is no message to the brain except one of contentment, the brain has no need to be active with disturbing thoughts, and is therefore ready for suggestions of a welcome nature.'[41]

Elman viewed the ability for the mind to become momentarily blank concerning a specific thing, i.e. temporary amnesia, as evidence of somnambulism. In fact, he argues that even if somnambulism has not yet been achieved, the suggestion and subsequent experience of amnesia can take patients into that state.

Elman's preferred means of achieving this amnesia was by having patients count backwards from 100, relaxing more with each number, until amnesia for the next number is experienced. There are downsides to this method, which we will discuss below, yet it remains an effective and reliable means of achieving temporary amnesia.

Cal Banyan recommends counting *up*, instead of down.[42] Part of his reasoning is that if you are counting down from 100 then people have a target – namely, the number 1 – to aim for. This may encourage them to keep counting, instead of reaching amnesia. However, if you count up then counting any further than a few numbers (as suggested by the hypnotist) becomes a futile endeavour, because the counting can keep going forever.

Despite Banyan's argument, I side with Elman in suggesting counting down. The main reason for my choice

---

41 ibid., p. 96.
42 See http://www.hypnosiscenter.com/free-article-elman-banyan-hypnotic-induction.htm

matches the argument of Larry Elman.[43] Counting up is an easy reflexive practice that it can be more difficult to stumble over. Similarly, counting down from, for example, 300 in groups of three may be too taxing a practice and encourage an over-focus on the numbers coming up next. Counting down from 100 is a good compromise that is neither too reflexive nor too taxing.

Having said that, anything can be used to demonstrate the blank mind expressed in amnesia. On rare occasions, some clients will struggle with forgetting the numbers, perhaps due to working with accounts, for example. In reality, this does not happen as often as is feared, but it is not unheard of.

On such occasions, therapeutic creativity would suggest going down a different route. In the permissive transcript above, I use the example of forgetting the letters in one's name when spelt backwards.

Relaxing the Numbers Away

Although this stage of the induction is often referred to as 'losing the numbers', such terminology is less than ideal. Again, for those who perhaps work with numbers, the idea of losing some numbers may initiate a subconscious rejection of the suggestion. Instead, Elman often speaks of 'relaxing the numbers away'. However, this carries its own problem.

Aphasia refers to an experience of being too relaxed to speak. If you do not face resistance to the suggestion of amnesia, *aphasia* is another hazard you may encounter. Simply put, this occurs when clients have not actually experienced a state of blank mind. They are simply too

43 Elman, H.L, (2011), pp. 33-35.

relaxed to keep counting out-loud. In my experience, you are far more likely to encounter this than a fear of losing the numbers, or an out-right rejection of the suggestion by accountants and others.

The difficulty for the hypnotist is that *aphasia* and amnesia can look exactly the same from the outside. It therefore becomes difficult to know for certain which situation you are facing. However, there are some clues to look our for.

If the induction has explicitly been one of progressive relaxation from the beginning – e.g. relax the eye-lids so much that they will not open – up to and including this point – e.g. relax those numbers away – then you are more likely to encounter aphasia. For this reason, at times you may want to use alternative language alongside suggestions for relaxation. Examples include mention of peace, calm, stillness, heaviness, contentment and so on.

If the client's counting of the numbers is slurred, or becomes slower or quieter with each number, it may be an indication that you are reaching *aphasia* instead of amnesia.

Finally, if the client exhales loudly and deeply in place of saying their final number out-loud then your client may be in a state of relaxation so deep that they experience an inability to speak out loud.

At times, Elman suggests that the experience of artificial somnambulism, seen in the demonstration of *aphasia* is a necessary stage in patients reaching genuine somnambulism. It therefore follows that aphasia is nothing to be feared by the prepared practitioner. There are, instead, a number of actions which can be taken to ensure that you are reaching genuine amnesia by suggestion.

As will be seen in the transcript following this chapter,

it is not enough to simply accept the client's silence as evidence of amnesia. Instead, you should explicitly ask them if the numbers have gone.

Secondly, you can employ a secondary amnesiac experience if you have doubts over the authenticity of the initial one. This time, you may choose to have the client forget letters of the alphabet, or how to spell their street name. The fact that they are able to keep speaking to follow the process again can reassure you that you are facing a genuine amnesia. Combine this with the explicit question over the removal of the letters/numbers and you can be confident that things are as they seem.

Finally, you may choose at this point to make use of the *Super Suggestion* spoken of below. If your client's response to the question, "Have they all gone?" leaves you unsure whether they have reached hypnotic amnesia or simply *aphasia*, the Super Suggestion can be employed following 'losing the numbers'.

EXERCISE

What is your understanding of the 'state' of somnambulism?

Regardless of whether or not is is a scientifically measurable state, do you find the concept useful?

If you do, are there other ways that we could describe it?

Is Zeig's distinction between Conditions, States and Moods helpful? Can it be utilised to present the experience of somnambulism in different ways?

Therapeutic Amnesia Transcript

The following transcript is from a time that the Elman induction was used as the beginning of a Therapeutic Induction.[44] The eye-lock used here is gratefully borrowed from James Hazlerig,[45] re-printed with permission.

You will notice that on this occasion, two different items were used for amnesia. There are a couple of reasons for this. Firstly, I had a suspicion that the client had not really achieved amnesia for the numbers, but was instead simply too relaxed to keep counting. So, I had them repeat the exercise, this time with letters. However, another reason that I repeated the amnesia portion of the process is that the client had already told me that their phobia made them feel "stupid". They repeated this word so often, both to me and internally to themselves, that I decided it would be a useful word to have them temporarily wipe from their mind.

The Beach scene was employed because the client had previously told me that the beach was their "special place", where they felt most comfortable and at home.

> Hypnotist: "Okay, well, when you are ready, you might want to begin by taking a nice long deep breath... fill up those lungs real good...

---

44 See The Anatomy of Inductions, for further discussion.
45 http://www.hypnosisaustin.com

And as you breathe out, you can just close your eyes... And relax. Getting rid of that surface tension in your body, letting your shoulders relax. And letting yourself go.

"Just let yourself get nice and comfortable. And any time that you want to move around and get more comfortable is perfectly fine.

"Continuing to relax, breathing in...and out... as if you are breathing in peace and calm and ... letting go of any stress and tension. That's it. Peace and Calm... Letting go.

"And as you've closed your eyes, you've entered a private space within your mind. And of course, when you go into a private room, it's perfectly natural to close the door, so as to block out any outside cares, worries, and concerns, just the way that you've closed your eyes down. And it's not unusual to then lock the door so that you can be safe and secure inside. You can do that metaphorically now by locking your eyelids shut. Now, after locking a door, it's natural to test it, tugging on the doorknob and finding it tightly locked shut. So when you're certain you've locked your eyelids shut, try in vain to open them, finding that the harder you attempt to open them, the more tightly locked they become.

"That's good. And as you stop testing those

eye-lids, you can relax and feel great. And the better you feel, the deeper you go. And the deeper you go, the better you feel.

"Now, I'd like to teach you how to reach a useful level of both physical and mental relaxation. So, that we are equipped to move forward and make positive changes for you, this very day. I would like you to experience, just how easily, naturally and quickly, you can do this.

"And every breath that you take, and every word that I say and every beat of your heart will cause you to go deeper and deeper into that state.

"And that same quality of relaxation that you have in your eyes can flow down now through your body from the top of your head to the tip of your toes. Letting go of every muscle, every fibre, every nerve... Floating, drifting, sinking down. That's it.

"Now, let's take this further. In a moment, not yet but in a moment, I will ask you to open and close your eyes. When you close your eyes, you can go back down and go ten times deeper. Want it to happen, and make it happen. Now go ahead and open your eyes... and close them... And go ten times deeper.

"In a moment, I'll ask you to open and close your eyes again. This time when you close your eyes, you can go twice as deep as you are right now. Doubling that physical relaxation... Go ahead and open your eyes... close your eyes... Twice as relaxed now. Double the relaxation, deeper and deeper.

"And in a moment, we will do this one more time... And notice how easily it occurs this time as you learn how simple this really is for you... Going as deep as you can go now. Alright, open your eyes... And... Way down... deeper down... let go. That's good. All the way.

"Okay, in a moment I am going to lift this arm [touches right wrist] and drop it. Don't try to help me or hinder me in any way... just let that arm hang there like a wet rag... [Picks up the wrist, moving it up and down and side to side slightly] That's right... and as I drop your arm down, you can go twice as deep as you are now... [Drop the arm] ...All the way down. Great...

"Okay, we have relaxed your body, so now let's relax your mind. In a moment, I'll ask you to slowly begin counting out loud, backwards, from 100. You will count like this:

[Saying numbers each time the client breathes out...] "100... 99... 98...

"And after each number, you can double your mental relaxation. And as you do that, you'll find that by the time you get to 97 or 96 you will have relaxed all of those numbers out of your mind. Want that... And you can have it.

"So, slowly begin counting backwards out loud, starting with 100..."

Client: "100"

H: "Double that relaxation."

C: "99"

H: "Deeper relaxed."

C: "98"

H: "Those numbers growing dim and distant..."

C: "97"

H: "Deeper relaxed."

C: "9..."

H: "And when you're ready, just push them

out. Just tell them to leave and they will go... And let them be gone."

H: "...Numbers all gone?"

C: "...Mmhmmm.."

H: "And now, let your mind drift to that Beach that you know so well... Find yourself there and take some time to familiarise yourself with your surroundings. Just notice whatever you notice. Maybe there are particular colours or sights that stand out to you. Perhaps there is the sound of waves, or children laughing, or anything else you can hear. Take some time to simply see what you see, hear what you hear and feel what you feel.

"And I wonder if you have ever written letters on the sand and watched as the sea washed them away.... or perhaps you've seen someone else do that, or you've seen something similar in movies, or on the television.

"Keeping that same level of relaxation, I wonder if you can imagine writing a word in the sand. I would like you to write it across the sand, so that the last letter is closest to the water and the first letter is closest to you.

"I would like you to write that word that you

call yourself when you used to feel that phobia. Write it out one letter at a time... It won't be there for long.

"Notice the texture of the sand, as you write. Perhaps it is warm from the heat of the Sun, or cool from the waves that have lapped it from time to time. Observe the sound that writing those letters makes.

"It may be that as you stretch out the word in the sand like that, that you see that it is merely a collection of letters, nothing more than a sound. Just like the sound of seagulls, or the sound of waves, sounds come and sounds go.

"And in a moment, I would like you to spell out the letters of that word for me, backwards, starting at the end. Like this...

"D... [wait for next exhalation]... I... And so on. And you can double that relaxation with each letter. And, as if to ensure that relaxation, every letter you spell will then be wiped away by the waves. And what you will find is that within just a few letters, you will have reached such a calm serene state that you will have relaxed the rest of those letters right out of your mind. Perhaps the waves will have wiped out the rest, or they will have just faded in the Sun... Want it and you can have it.

"So, go ahead now and begin to spell out that word backwards, doubling your relaxation with each letter."

C: "D"

H: "Doubling that relaxation..."

C: "I"

H: "Letters fading away..."

C: "P"

H: "Deeper relaxed..."

C: [Silence]

H: "All gone?"

C: "Yeah."

H: "That's good."

EXERCISE

Think of various items that you could use for the amnesia section of the Elman induction. What are the benefits or disadvantages of them?

Practice the Elman induction, using different things for amnesia and note which items your practice partner seems to forget most easily.

Experiment with describing the amnesia in different ways – relaxing away the numbers, wiping letters off of a blackboard, watching the number float away on a cloud, etc. - and see which are most helpful for your clients and most natural for you.

GRAHAM OLD

The Super Suggestion

This is not an aspect of the Induction as originally taught by Elman himself. However, I have found it to be a beneficial addition that fits naturally within the process. My recommendation is to include it after the suggestion for amnesia, or even as part of the amnesia stage to enable you to distinguish between genuine amnesia and *aphasia*.

I first discovered the useful tool known as the 'Super Suggestion' in the writings of Jonathan Chase.[46] However, Chase suggests that it was known at least as early as 1867.

The fact is that if you are seeking to reach a place where your client is most open to responding to your suggestions, then it makes sense to simply suggest that they follow your suggestions. However, use this too early and you risk a rejection. After all, it is the hypnotic equivalent of asking someone to agree to whatever you ask of them before you say it. If you have not already established a 'deep' enough state of consent then the Super Suggestion may be rejected and you can even find yourself retreating a few steps back up the pyramid.

The Super Suggestion, as I encountered it, comes from the realm of Stage Hypnosis. However, it need not be restricted to that arena. If you have cascaded your

---

46 See Jonathan Chase, *Deeper and Deeper*, p. 101.

suggestions and seen a progressive increase of consent, relaxation and selective thinking then the Super Suggestion can function to make explicit the client's engagement with the process so far.

The following example of a Super Suggestion is as blunt as that employed in a Stage Hypnosis[47] or Street Hypnosis[48] scenario. However, it fits comfortably within the Elman process and is designed to avoid any kind of rejection by your clients:

> From this moment on, you can accept everything I say to you, every single thing I say. Everything I say will instantly become your reality. You will know what I say you know, feel what I say you feel and do what I ask you to do. Everything I say is instantly your reality without doubt, question or hesitation because you have such a powerful mind. You can follow perfectly every direction I give you.
>
> Just nod your head to let me know you understand and accept this suggestion.

This, like all suggestions, benefits from repetition. After having repeated the suggestion two or three times, I find it helpful to ask the client to visibly accept the suggestion by nodding their head.

Of course, it is possible to develop less authoritarian versions of the Super Suggestion. These may make it less fitting for a Stage/Street situation, but perhaps more

47 ibid., p. 101.
48 Anthony Jacquin, *Reality is Plastic*, p. 70.

acceptable in a therapeutic environment:

> And you have done so well, that from this moment on, you are free to accept everything I say to you. Everything I say can instantly become your reality. As you have shown yourself to have a powerful subconscious mind, you can – when you are ready – allow yourself to know what I say you can know, feel what I suggest you can feel and you can find yourself able to do what I ask you to do.

> Knowing that you are here for your good, and that you have taken the decision to regain control of your life – and demonstrated that you have the resources to do so – everything I say can instantly become your reality without doubt, question or hesitation... because you have such a powerful mind... you can follow perfectly every direction I give you.

> And you can nod your head when you are ready to let me know that you understand and embrace this suggestion.

EXERCISE

The Super Suggestion is not a part of the induction as originally taught by Dave Elman.

Do you find its inclusion helpful or not?

Are there other ways to present something like the Super Suggestion which might make it more acceptable to your clients?

For example, rather than saying, "you will accept everything I say", experiment with suggestions like, "And I just wonder how easy you will find it to accept everything that is suggested to you, for your good."

Is the Super Suggestion an alternative to somnambulism, or can the two ideas work together?

Summary of the Process

Let's take a look at the summary again. This time we will use the more accurate descriptions, as suggested by Larry Elman.

- Pre-talk
- Catalepsy of a group of small muscles, to bypass critical faculty
- Deepening
- Fractionation
- Catalepsy of a group of large muscles
- Amnesia by suggestion

As you can see from the numerous transcripts provided throughout this book, appreciating the flow of the process and moving away from a static script allows greater freedom and flexibility.

EXERCISE

Now that you are familiar with the process, are there any parts that you would change?

Do you feel comfortable with the order of the various parts of the induction, or would you prefer to move things around?

Would you prefer the Super Suggestion be included as a staple element in the induction, or left as an optional added extra?

The Esdaile Coma State

As we are discussing Elman, it makes sense to briefly mention the Esdaile state. However, this is not a necessary part of the Elman Induction, which was designed as a tool to reliably lead someone into somnambulism.

In the 19th Century, the Scottish surgeon James Esdaile was using hypnosis whilst working in India. Esdaile submitted reports in 1846 claiming that he had performed several thousand minor operations and about 300 major ones, including 19 amputations, all painlessly. It is also reported that Esdaile reduced the post-operative fatality rate from 50% down to below 10%, due to a lessening of post-operative shock.

On his return to Scotland, Esdaile was unable to duplicate such a success rate. This is sometimes felt to be a result of his status and the levels of expectation and belief that he was able to generate in India, whilst in the West he was treated with a more objective medical scrutiny. It may also reflect the fact that, in India, Esdaile could achieve such deep states of hypnosis over a prolonged period of time.

Approximately one century later, Dave Elman was familiar with what some came to call the "hypnotic coma" from his work as a Stage Hypnotist. He mentions the embarrassment that could be caused to the hypnotist, when they encountered those rare subjects who would sit slumped in the chair, unresponsive to any suggestions. The stage operators at times even had to devise ways to rouse someone from this deep state and would keep such secrets to themselves, so as to elevate themselves above their rivals. Elman devised his own effective means of doing this, which we will turn to below, based upon his observations and understanding of the experiences of his subjects.

Elman wisely referred to this level of hypnosis as the "Esdaile state", dropping the common 'coma' description. This reflected his intention to have hypnosis taken seriously by the medical community. Additionally, both Stage Hypnotists and the general public feared the coma state as an accidental and unproductive state of being that it could be difficult to rouse someone out of.

Taking Someone into Esdaile

Elman's method for leading someone into the Esdaile state is remarkably simple. By this point, this should not surprise anyone, as it is clear that Elman had a positive bias towards methods which were simple, direct and effective. The thing that is unique about Elman's approach is that he was able to reach the Esdaile state in a relatively brief amount of time. On top of that, he was able to do so intentionally and eventually with a predictable level of success.

Here is Elman's description of taking someone into Esdaile, having previously brought them down to somnambulism.

As I remember, I spoke to the patient more or

less like this: "I know how relaxed you are, but even in your relaxed state I'll bet you sense in your own mind that there is a state of relaxation below the one you're in right now. Can you sense that?"

The patient answered, "Yes."

I continued, "You know that you can clench your fist and make it tighter and tighter and tighter - and you might call that the height of tension. You can relax the same fist until you can't relax it any more. You might call that the basement of relaxation. I'm going to try to take you down to the basement.

"To get down to floor A, you have to relax twice as much as you have relaxed already. To get down to floor B, you have to relax twice as much as you did at floor B, and to get down to C, you have to relax twice as much as you did at floor B. But when you reach floor C, that is the basement of relaxation, and at that point you will give off signs by which I will be able to tell that you are at the basement. You don't know what these signs are, and I'm not going to tell you what they are, but every person who has ever been at the basement of relaxation gave off those signs ... Let's get started.

"You will ride down to floor A on an imaginary

elevator and you will use that same elevator to get down to the basement of relaxation. You are on that elevator now. When I snap my fingers, that elevator will start down. If you relax twice as much as you have relaxed already you will be down at floor A. Tell me when you are at floor A by saying the letter A out loud."

In about thirty seconds, he murmured "A" in an almost indistinguishable voice. I followed a similar procedure, taking him down to floor B. It was almost impossible for him to say the letter B out loud, but he formed the sound with his lips. When he reached floor C, he was unable to speak, and not a muscle moved.'[49]

This is not the only way to achieve the Esdaile State intentionally, though most alternate routes are effectively variations of this. I make use of a common staircase deepener, which can be seen in the Appendix.

Signs of Depth

It will be clear by now that 'signs of depth' is perhaps best understood as a metaphorical description. However, it is the terminology chosen by Elman and common in literature on the topic.

Elman felt that there were a number of signs that someone was in the 'hypnotic coma' and used the following tests to demonstrate this.

---

49 Elman (1977), pp.125-126.

Anesthesia

It is believed that when someone is 'at floor C', then you have automatic anesthesia. So, without giving any warning, Elman would take a pair of Allis clamps or towel clips and test for anesthesia.

Moving an arm or a leg

The next test was to ask the patient to try to move an arm or leg. If they are unable to do so, then they are ready for the third test.

Opening eyes

Thirdly, you ask your client to try to open their eyes. In somnambulism, when they try to open their eyes, you will often see a movement of the muscles, or raising of the eyebrows. In Esdaile, the surrounding tiny muscles do not work at all and you should see no movement.

Catatonia

The fourth test should be for catatonia. It is not suggested, but achieved automatically.

Elman rightly notes that catatonia can be obtained in the lightest state of hypnosis. Therefore, it only actually functions as a sign of depth if it is carried out in the correct order. According to the model, when a client passes all of these four tests *in the exact order given*, you can be sure you have the true hypnotic coma, and can proceed from there. You should not go on to a new test, until your client has passed the previous one.

Emergence from the Coma State

Elman discovered an interesting fact regarding the Esdaile state, from interviewing those who had been there. Rather than being a zombie-like state of inability to respond, Elman learned that the Esdaile state was a euphoric experience. It seems that the reason people did not respond when in the Esdaile state is simply because it felt better not to.

> Rather than being a state which is to be avoided, we found that patients described it as "the best state of hypnosis there is. It's wonderful. I don't know when I was so beautifully relaxed."

> ...The coma brings with it a complete and entire euphoria. Rather than allow themselves to be disturbed, when anyone gave them a pain impulse, they completely disregarded it, thereby giving themselves complete general anesthesia.[50]

Using Elman's method to reach the Esdaile state, it is a rather logical process to rouse someone. You simply ask them to come up to Level B. When they are at Level B, bring them back up to level A. From there, bring them up to somnambulism and you can then exit your hypnosis session as you would normally.

---

50 ibid., p. 129.

However, if a hypnotist was to find themselves with a client who accidentally slipped into the hypnotic coma, then we have an ingenious means of rousing them. The following simple method was apparently devised by Elman's wife, Pauline, and has worked for me every time that I have used it. Simply whisper in your client's ear:

"If you don't open your eyes when I tell you to, you can never have this state again."[51]

As the Esdaile state is routinely described as an enjoyable, even euphoric state, this suggestion informs the client that you appreciate the level of their experience, but that you need them to come out of it, so that they can go back in at a later date.

---

51 ibid., p. 134.

EXERCISE

Continue to practice the Elman induction.

By now, you should be able to proceed with some speed. This does not need to feel abrupt to your client, but can actually increase the credibility of the induction. It can give a real sense that something out of the ordinary is happening.

Practice taking your clients all of the way through the process, including into the Esdaile state.

If the 'depth' of Esdaile concerns you, feel free to jump ahead to the trouble-shooting section, before you proceed.

Trouble-Shooting and FAQ

They open their eyes

The earliest difficulty you may encounter with the Elman induction is that you client opens their eyes following your suggestion that they stay shut. There are a number of reasons why this may happen.

Firstly, they may simply not have understood your suggestion properly. It is reasonable that they believed you expected them to try as hard as they could to open their eyes, so they did. They went right ahead and opened their eyes! This situation is easily rectified by saying something like, "Well done. You've demonstrated that you *can* open your eyes. As I said, you remain in control at all times. <u>Now, I want you to demonstrate that you *can't* open your eyes</u>. So, go ahead and close your eyes again and relax them so well that they are just too relaxed to open. And then demonstrate to yourself that you've relaxed them that well by keeping hold of that relaxation whilst you try in vain to open them."

A second reason that someone may open their eyes is fear. Despite a positive pre-talk, they may still equate not being able to open their eyes with being controlled by you. In that case, you can proceed with a more permissive version of the eye-lock (see the Permissive Transcript, or the Therapeutic Amnesia Transcript), or use something other than their eyes.

Some people really benefit from being able to see their own catalepsy. So, you might choose to have them watch, whilst their finger stays glued to their leg. However, if you do move on from an eye-lock to something else, it is important not to give the impression that they have failed. Say something like, "Good. You've demonstrated that you are able to stay in control, just as I said you would. And now I would like to use that powerful mind of yours to show you something really interesting..."

I would argue that *failure to understand* and *fear* are the two main reasons that someone may open their eyes. Another reason this sometimes happens is that someone feels like you are challenging them and they do not like to lose. In that case, simply reframe things as above and then repeat the suggestion, this time making the Priority of Thought clear.

Their arm is not heavy

Another fairly common issue when you are first learning to use the Elman induction is that when you lift up your client's arm, it is not heavy, or does not drop down. There are a couple of ways to tackle this.

The first thing I do is tell them not to help me. I would say something like, "No, let *me* lift it" or, "Don't help me. Just relax it completely". As I am saying that, I may gently sway their arm from side to side, by the wrist, as if I am shaking the tension out. This kinaesthetically reiterates to them what a loose and relaxed arm would feel like.

The second way to address this comes up if their arm does not drop when you let it go. As with their eyes popping open above, when you have told them they will not, this can be because they sensed a challenge in what you were saying. Alternatively, they may not be sure what was expected of them. In cases like this, you should again avoid implying failure and either lower their arm and repeat the suggestion, or switch to a stiff-arm.

My preference, as their arm is already up in the air – and they may be responding to a presumed challenge – is to congratulate them and reframe the occasion into a stiff-arm catalepsy by saying something like:

> "Excellent. Now, I'm going to take your arm and I want you to extend it and make a fist. That's it." [Taps end of fist.]

> "Now, make it rigid as I count to three. Make that so rigid you can't bend it. One – make it rigid – two, like steel – three, solid. Now when you know that that arm is unbendable, you can't bend it no matter how hard you try. Just go ahead and try and bend that arm and find that it just won't bend.

> "Now you can stop trying... And as I shake the arm like this [shaking arm by the wrist] it just becomes limp and loose and relaxed, like a wet dishcloth... That's it.

> "And as I drop your arm into your lap, you can just go even deeper... [drops arm] ...all the way down."

If you find that you regularly face the issue of your client's arm not being heavy, it is worth examining what you say before you pick their arm up. It may be that you are not clear enough in saying what you expect to happen. Remember, that this is about achieving catalepsy *by suggestion*. So, you might want to pre-empt this stage by saying something like:

> "I'm now going to lift your left arm up by the wrist and if you've followed the instructions up to this point – and I think you have done really well – that arm will just be loose and limp like a wet dish cloth and will just drop into your lap when I let go."

The numbers won't go

This is perhaps the most feared problem that comes up for people using the Elman induction, especially if they have been trained to approach it like a script. Thankfully, it is by no means insurmountable and there are a number of things that you can do if your client struggles to 'lose the numbers.'

Firstly, you may want to explore your terminology. 'Losing the numbers' is not a desirable description and perhaps provokes the concern that you will not be able to find them again. Preferable language might speak of 'letting the numbers go' or 'relaxing them away'.

Whilst we are talking about the numbers, when you ask your client if they have gone, it may help not to draw their attention back to them. So, instead of asking (in a voice that reveals uncertainty), "Have the numbers gone?", you can ask, "Are they gone?" Or, even, "Have they gone yet?"

Another approach is to use something as an alternative to forgetting numbers. You can have someone forget letters from their name, or how to spell a word, for example. This may be especially useful if you are working with those for whom keeping track of the numbers is an essential task.

Having said that, this reason for failing to achieve amnesia comes up far less often than concerned hypnotists, or inexperienced trainers, may assume. More often than not, the issue is due more to the congruity and delivery of the hypnotist, than the engagement of the patient.

Nevertheless, I have found that the approach used by Elman is a reliable and effective way to address the issue of stubborn numbers:

> Elman: [to doctors] Let me show you again the technique I use when the numbers don't disappear. I lift his hand and say, "When I drop your hand the lights will go out and you won't see any more numbers... There you are... The lights are out and all the numbers are gone..."[52]

In effect, this is a slight pattern-interrupt, followed by alternative visualisation. It is fairly common that the reason someone struggles to achieve amnesia is not so much because of a resistance to losing the numbers, but because of a failure to fully understand your directions. In such instances, a different approach to the same goal is recommended.

As well as the visualisation used by Elman, you might have them picture numbers floating away on clouds, or

---

52 ibid., p. 113.

numbers on a TV screen getting smaller and smaller, or further and further away.

Related to the issue of not fully understanding your directions, some clients will need you to be more explicit. They may not fully appreciate how amnesia is to be reached, or what it would feel like. So, I may at times employ descriptions like, "...the way that someone's name can be on the tip of your tongue, but you just can't find it..." or "Like when you know that you know an actor's name and you stumble around in your mind but you just can't grasp it. You know you know it, but right now it is just out of your reach, just on the tip of your tongue, but you can't quite get it..."

Finally, another approach is to adopt a more abrupt pattern-interrupt. This is especially useful if you suspect that their conscious mind has become too pre-occupied with keeping the numbers and resists letting them go. In such a situation you might choose to switch to something like the 8-word induction[53], before carrying on with the Super Suggestion.

Why do you say, "Are the numbers gone?"

Some trainers teach that you should never say, "Are the numbers gone?" as this makes your client remember them again. Yet, you'll see in one of the transcripts that we have said this.

The truth is, your client is forgetting certain numbers. They are not forgetting that it is numbers they are forgetting. That is, they are not forgetting the concept of Numbers themselves. So, it follows that simply using the word "numbers" should not cause you any problems.

---

53 See http://howtodoinductions.com/inductions/8word

Having said that, if you are regularly encountering problems with number amnesia, or you suspect that a particular client will, then avoiding the word might help. However, in such circumstances, you may simply find it easier to have them forget something else, like how to spell their family name backwards.

Are they just too relaxed to speak?

We discussed above, the risks of mistaking aphasia for amnesia. As stated there, this is particularly a risk if every part of the induction has been framed as an exercise in relaxation. In such circumstances, it can help to avoid describing the amnesia as "relaxing the numbers" away.

The issue of aphasia is the reason that you do not take your client's silence as evidence of amnesia. You need to explicitly ask them if the numbers have gone. If, instead of saying their final number they sigh deeply, or do not respond to your question, then you are likely to be at a place of aphasia, not amnesia.

The natural way to respond in such a situation, is simply to have them forget a second item. It can be beneficial, in my experience, to incorporate a visual element to the second item, so that it is not simply a repetition of the earlier attempt at amnesia. You might have them wipe letters off of a blackboard, or see numbers floating away on a cloud.

Is it genuine amnesia?

Some people may wonder if the amnesia we see in the

Elman Induction is genuine amnesia. For example, Melissa Tiers has recently questioned whether or not the hypnotee may simply be too relaxed to recall their numbers.[54]

It is necessary to point out that being too relaxed to speak (i.e. aphasia) is not the same as being too relaxed to recall the numbers. If someone is simply so relaxed that they are ignoring the suggestion to count out-loud, then you have reached a hurdle in the Elman process. It is by no means an insurmountable barrier and we have provided ways to address this above. However, it does demonstrate to the hypnotist that the process is not proceeding as planned. In short, your client is not following your suggestions.

However, if as a result of your suggestions, your client has become so relaxed that they cannot mentally locate which number comes next in the sequence, I would see that as a useful signal that they are following your suggestions and the process is progressing as hoped.

It may be helpful to recognise that hypnotic amnesia is rarely amnesia in the genuine sense of that word. Whether on a stage or in a therapy room, it is usually temporary amnesia, achieved by suggestion. The client manages to use their mind in such a way that it cannot – or will not – recall certain information. So, it seems something of a red herring to me to debate whether the amnesia seen in the Elman induction is the real thing. As long as it is as a result of suggestion – and not merely the client being too relaxed to bother opening their mouth – I would not concern yourself with whether or not they have genuinely forgotten something, or are just too relaxed to

---

54 Tiers, M. (2010). Integrative Hypnosis. USA: Melissa Tiers. Pp. 68-69.

recall it. They may be one and the same thing.

Why don't you believe in Somnambulism?

It's not that we do not (or do) believe in somnambulism. It's more a case that we don't believe a particular understanding of levels of hypnosis or depth of trance should be a hindrance to learning and employing a useful induction.

I believe you can still put the Elman Induction to good use, even if you hold to a different understanding of hypnosis than that of Dave Elman.

At the end of the day, greater minds than I have debated this question for many years – and continue to do so. I do not believe our practice of hypnosis should wait on the sidelines for them to come to a consensus or solid conclusion.

Moreover, I believe that the benefits that are associated with the state of somnambulism are the desired result, not the state in and of itself.

What is the benefit of the Esdaile state?

How someone answers this question would depend on their view of hypnotic states and what the Esdaile state actually entails. For Elman, Esdaile was a euphoric state that contained the automatic experience of anesthesia, without suggestion. That would make it beneficial to doctors and dentists, whilst being highly desirable to patients.

Can you communicate with the Esdaile state?

One supposed downside of the Esdaile state is the coma-like inactivity of its participants. However, with some forethought, it is far from impossible to communicate with clients in the coma state. There are a couple of ways to achieve this.

Essentially, you will want to inform your clients – before they reach the Esdaile state – that they will still be able to communicate with you when they are there. A simple way to do this is through ideomotor response signals, where for example they raise their left forefinger for "Yes" and their right forefinger for "No".

Some practitioners find it helpful to tell clients that some part of them will remain in somnambulism, whilst the rest of them goes into the Esdaile state. It seems very unlikely to me that different parts of the same body will be in different hypnotic 'states.' However, it is a helpful metaphor to convey to clients the idea that part of them will still be able to respond.

Should you deepen before going into Esdaile?

Some trainers teach that it is beneficial to use a deepener in-between somnambulism and the Esdaile state. I do not see that this is necessary and in fact it could be seen as questioning the nature of what is being experienced. If somnambulism really is the state that its proponents claim that it is and if Esdaile is the coma state that Elman believed it was, then there is no necessary deepener between the two states. According to Elman, there is no way to go deeper than somnambulism, except by going into Esdaile.

Nevertheless, I often recommend using something like the Super Suggestion following the loss of numbers. This ensures that even if somnambulism had not been reached, you now have a sufficient level of consent with which to proceed. Regardless of your model of hypnosis, I suppose there is no harm in viewing the inclusion of the Super Suggestion at this stage as 'deepening' the client's experience.

EXERCISE

Contact us at www.howtodoinductions.com

if you have any ongoing questions which have not been answered.

Final Thoughts

The Elman Induction is a reliable and effective means of leading people in to a deep experience of hypnosis. Rather than being simply a script to follow, it is a flexible and adaptable process that will richly reward the practitioner who takes the time to fully acquaint themselves with it.

As I have stated repeatedly, it is not necessary to understand the finer details of the induction in the precise way that Dave Elman did. Yet, I do not say this to disregard Elman's interpretation. Instead, it is my intention to make his induction accessible to as wide an audience as possible, regardless of any preconceived models or schools of thought.

The following books, DVDs and websites are offered as valuable resources in deepening your understanding and practice of this unique induction.

Hypnotherapy by Dave Elman

Hailed as a classic in its field, Dave Elman's *Hypnotherapy* is a forceful and dynamic presentation of hypnosis as a direct and effective tool. *Hypnotherapy* is a culmination of information and practical applications gathered from over a decade of Elman teaching Physicians and Dentists his 10 Lesson Course on Hypnosis and its uses in Medicine.

Blueprint of the Dave Elman Induction by H. Larry Elman

Dave Elman's son, Colonel Larry Elman makes a compelling case for viewing the Elman Induction as a process, not a script. In a very real sense, this current book can be seen as a commentary on Larry Elman's discussion of his father's induction.

The Dave Elman Induction 2-DVD Set by Sean Michael Andrews / Don Patterson

This DVD set explains in-depth how to use the Dave Elman Induction. It takes you through the entire induction, step-by-step, from the moment you meet the subject, all the way through to deepening the trance and emerging the subject. The level of detail will ensure that you can perform this induction confidently and effectively.

This set includes never before published information about Dave Elman and his induction. Larry Elman joins Sean to discuss how the induction was developed, how it was taught and why it is still the most effective induction ever.

Best Practices of Dave Elman 4-DVD Set by Sean Michael Andrews and H. Larry Elman

Think of this as a DVD version of Dave Elman's book, featuring two of his most accomplished and knowledgeable students. Contents include waking hypnosis, hypnosis with children, pain management, deepeners, breaking the hypnotic seal, regression to cause hypnotherapy, how to induce the Esdaile state, and more.

Integrative Hypnosis by Melissa Tiers

Drawing directly from Melissa's dynamic live teaching sessions, *Integrative Hypnosis* takes the reader on an inspirational and practical journey through the most powerful change techniques, combining: Classical and Ericksonian hypnosis, Neuro Linguistic Programming, Cognitive, Behavioural and Energy Psychology. Containing demonstrations, metaphors and hypnotic language patterns, this simple and accessible book brings to life Melissa's exciting and infectious teaching approach.

www.hypnothoughts.com

HypnoThoughts is the web's leading forum for all things related to hypnosis and hypnotherapy. Members include leading thinkers and practitioners in the world of hypnosis. An incredibly valuable resource – and it's free!

www.howtodoinductions.com

As you would expect, we would recommend our free inductions site as the premier website for learning about inductions.

Our web-site offers transcripts of various inductions, from classics like the Progressive Muscle Relaxation to the Bandler Handshake and others. New inductions are added - and annotated - regularly, but only after they have been assessed as useful and achievable for beginners and experts alike.

www.briefhypnosis.com

Brief Hypnosis run live trainings in Therapeutic Inductions, offering hands-on experience in creating solution-focused inductions on-the-fly. You will learn principles and techniques that are not often taught elsewhere, which will take your confidence, creativity and client-base to completely new levels.

Sign-up for the newsletter at howtodoinductions.com to stay informed.

EXERCISE

Continue to practice the Elman Induction...

That's it!

Reading a book will not guarantee that you can make the most of this induction any more than a DVD on swimming will prepare you for the Sea.

Practice. Practice. Practice.

And then practice with a partner! Again and again and again...

GRAHAM OLD

Appendix

The following transcript demonstrates an alternative way to take someone into the Esdaile state. It begins at the point after number amnesia has been successfully reached.

Alternative Esdaile Transcript

Hypnotist: All I am going to do now is ask you to imagine that you are at the top of grand staircase, that winds down to the left or the right, with a banister for you to hold on to. And at the bottom of the staircase, there is a door. I don't know what colour that door is, but behind the door is a place of peace and calm, safety and serenity. You might think of it as your special place, that your mind has subconsciously chosen to allow you to relax and be free there.

This flight of stairs has ten steps. And you are at the top of the staircase. In a moment, you will begin to move down the staircase, doubling your relaxation with ever step.

When you get to the bottom of the staircase, you can open that doorway and step through to your special place, that place of calm and relaxation.

So, moving down now from the tenth step, [wait for their exhalation] to the ninth step... doubling that relaxation with every step.

Moving down now to... [wait for their exhalation] eight... deeper and deeper...

[wait for their exhalation] Seven... Going further and further down.

[wait for their exhalation] Six...

[wait for their exhalation] Five... Deeper and deeper.

[wait for their exhalation] Four...

[wait for their exhalation] Three... Moving effortlessly down...

[wait for their exhalation] Three... Double that relaxation.

[wait for their exhalation] Two... Almost

164

there...

And... [wait for their exhalation] One...

So, now you can open that door and walk through to your special place... Take some time to walk around and notice whatever you notice. There may be particular colours that stand out to you. Or sounds that you didn't expect to hear... Just see what you see, hear what you hear and feel what you feel.

And as you enjoy that place of peace and calm, I would like you to look around. Because somewhere there you will find a doorway, or a staircase, or a transporter to a *deep* place of hypnosis. Take some time to look around and when you find it, just nod your head to let me know.

Client: [Client nods]

H: Now take that journey to that place of deep hypnosis and when you get there, say, "I'm here."

C: "I'm here."

H: And you can take some time now to enjoy that deep place of hypnosis. For all I know, it looks just like your previous place, but is an even deeper experience. Just see what you see, hear what you hear and feel what you feel.

And as you enjoy that place of peace and calm, I would like you to look around. Because very soon you will find a doorway, or a staircase, or a transporter to a *deeper* place of hypnosis. Take some time to look around and when you find it, just nod your head to let me know.

C: [Client nods]

H: So, take that journey to that place of deeper hypnosis and when you get there, say, "I'm here."

C: [Answers slowly...] "...ere."

H: Take some time now to enjoy that deep place of hypnosis. It may look just like your previous place, but it is an even deeper experience. Or it may be somewhere new. Just see what you see, hear what you hear and feel what you feel.

And as you enjoy that place, I would like you to look around. Because very soon you will find a doorway, or a staircase, or a transporter to the *deepest* place of hypnosis. Take some time to look around and when you find it, just nod your head to let me know.

C: [Client nods]

H: So, take the journey to that place of deepest hypnosis... when you're there, say, "I'm here."

C: [Client remains silent, but exhales deeply through their nose, as their head and shoulders slump down.]

GRAHAM OLD

Bibliography

Chase, J. (2000). *Deeper and Deeper*. Devon: Academy of Hypnotic Arts.

Chase, J. (2007). *Don't Look in His Eyes*. Devon: Academy of Hypnotic Arts.

Elman, D. (1977). *Hypnotherapy*. Glendale, CA: Westwood Publishing Co.

Elman, H. L. (2011). *Blueprint of the Dave Elman Induction*. Henderson, NC: Dave Elman Hypnosis Institute.

Jacquin, A. (2007). *Reality is Plastic*. Derby: UKHTC.

James, T. (2000). *Hypnosis: A Comprehensive Guide*. Carmarthen: Crown House Publishing.

Lynn, S. & Rhue, J. Eds. (1991) *Theories of Hypnosis: Current Models and Perspectives*. New York: Guilford Press.

Nash, M. & Barnier, A., eds. (2008). *The Oxford Handbook of Hypnosis: Theory, Research, and Practice*. Oxford: OUP.

McGill, O. (1996). *The New Encyclopedia of Stage Hypnotism*. Carmarthen: Crown House Publishing.

Nongard, R. (2007). *Inductions and Deepeners: Styles and Approaches for Effective Hypnosis*. Andover, KS: Peach Tree Professional Education.

Old, G. (2014). *Mastering the Leisure Induction*. Milton Keynes: 61 Books.

Old, G. (2016). *Revisiting Hypnosis*. Milton Keynes: 61 Books.

Patterson, D. *"The Dave Elman Induction"* [DVD]. The Atlantic Hypnosis Institute.

Tiers, M. (2010). *Integrative Hypnosis*. USA: Melissa Tiers.

Zeig, J. (2014). *The Induction of Hypnosis*. Phoenix, AZ: The Milton H. Erickson Foundation Press.

About the Author

Graham Old is a Solution-focused Hypnotist from the United Kingdom. A Graduate of Spurgeon's College, London and the University of Wales, Graham is a former University Chaplain and Community Pastor and remains an active participant of local peace and justice campaigns. He has experience as a Father's Worker and Assistant Social Worker, as well as working in private clinical practice and running the most popular inductions site on the web.

Graham is a popular conference speaker, writer and trainer, with over two decades experience teaching meditation and self-hypnosis. He is an insightful presence in contemporary hypnosis and the developer of the acclaimed *Therapeutic Inductions* approach.

Made in United States
North Haven, CT
20 October 2022

25704150R00098